THE
PHILOSOPHY
OF
SCIENCE

THE SYSTEMS, VALIDITY, AND ETHICS OF SCIENTIFIC INQUIRY

THE
PHILOSOPHY
OF
SCIENCE

THE SYSTEMS, VALIDITY, AND ETHICS OF SCIENTIFIC INQUIRY

EDITED BY MARIE WAHL

Britannica
Educational Publishing

Published in 2014 by Britannica Educational Publishing (a trademark of Encyclopædia Britannica, Inc.) in association with The Rosen Publishing Group, Inc.
29 East 21st Street, New York, NY 10010

Distributed exclusively by Rosen Publishing.
To see additional Britannica Educational Publishing titles, go to rosenpublishing.com

First Edition

Britannica Educational Publishing
J.E. Luebering: Director, Core Reference Group
Anthony L. Green: Editor, Compton's by Britannica

Rosen Educational Services
Hope Lourie Killcoyne: Executive Editor
Marie Wahl: Editor
Nelson Sá: Art Director
Brian Garvey: Designer, cover design
Cindy Reiman: Photography Manager
Nicole Baker: Photo Research
Introduction by Adam Augustyn

Library of Congress Cataloging-in-Publication Data

The philosophy of science: the systems, validity, and ethics of scientific inquiry/editor, Marie Wahl.
    pages cm. — (Scientific inquiry: concepts, methods, and theories)
Includes bibliographical references and index.
ISBN 978-1-62275-113-6 (library binding)
1. Science—Philosophy. I. Wahl, Marie, editor of compilation.
Q175.3.P53 2014
501—dc23
                                                                    2013021538

Manufactured in the United States of America

CONTENTS

2

39

44

62

74

86

An association between such seemingly disparate academic fields as philosophy and science may strike some as incongruous. Philosophy is one of the oldest disciplines of what is widely known as the humanities, a grouping that traditionally does not include the sciences. There is a disconnect between the very concepts upon which the fields (as broadly defined) focus; humanities are concerned with the culture and values of human beings, while science centres on the natural world. In fact, most American universities and colleges separate the two fields into completely different schools, namely, the arts and the sciences.

However, as this book illustrates, philosophy and science are inextricably linked. Indeed, they share a long history. In ancient Western civilizations, nascent scientists were known as "natural philosophers," as the lines between the two fields were blurred. Lacking the advanced investigative methods that came about later in history, early "scientists" had to plumb the natural world in their own minds via observation, reasoning, and abstractions. Even as science grew into a more outwardly focused field, the relationship between the two remained as philosophers continued to account for the aims and methods of the sciences.

A philosopher, Theophrastus, teaching students. Theophrastus was the successor of Aristotle, one of the great early scientists, or "natural philosophers." British Library/Robana/Hulton Fine Art Collection /Getty Images

While noted scientific minds such as Francis Bacon, Galileo, Isaac Newton, and Albert Einstein all contributed insights into the character of science during their lives, the study of the philosophy of science truly came into its own in the early 20th century. That was when groups of philosophers began to make concerted efforts to treat the investigation of the elements of scientific inquiry as a distinct discipline in and of itself, and not just as an addendum to other scientific pursuits. One of the first such efforts came from a group of European philosophers who came to be known as the logical positivists. These individuals aimed to formulate a universal "logic of the sciences" that would correspond to the logic of mathematics. The positivists aimed to find agreed-upon criteria of meaningfulness (or "cognitive significance") to implement their goals but were thwarted by proposals that were either too severe or too lax. Thereafter the group evolved to embrace a more temperate movement known as logical empiricism, which undertook a less-rigid search for a logical theory of scientific method.

One of the notable problems tackled by the logical empiricists and other philosophical schools was that of understanding scientific justification. In the face of the question as to whether or not there are particular conditions that underlie all bodies of evidence that support scientific hypotheses, the logical empiricists looked for a "logic of confirmation" that would identify those conditions. Two of philosophy's most notable empiricists, Rudolf Carnap and Carl Hempel, made significant contributions to the field in their attempts to solve the problem. Despite the pair's ultimate failing to do so, Carnap's work in particular argued persuasively for a correlation between the degree to which a hypothesis can be confirmed and the probability that a body of evidence supports it.

Philosophic explorations of probabilities and confirmations are by no means solely creations of the 20th century. In fact, the most prominent current method of approaching the problem had been developed by the 18th-century English mathematician Thomas Bayes. Bayesianism revolves around the idea that acquiring evidence will modify the probability that has been deductively ascribed to a hypothesis. His contemporary followers have been divided into "objective" Bayesians, who believe that there are objective criteria for assigning probabilities, and the much more prevalent "subjective" Bayesians, who believe that such criteria do not exist. According to the subjective Bayesians, the goal of a philosophical inquiry into a hypothesis is not to prove the "truth" of the hypothesis but to assign probabilities to rational inquiries that are then adjusted accordingly as evidence is collected.

An alternative to subjective Bayesianism, known as eliminativism, was developed in an effort to take into account the acceptance and rejection of hypotheses to better mirror the scientific practice of testing and eliminating rival hypotheses, as opposed to systematically revising the probabilities of those hypotheses. One of the most important eliminativists was Karl Popper, who believed that even tentative hypotheses that have survived the eliminative process are worthy of being pursued since—even though the survival of a hypotheses through a series of tests does not necessarily make it "true"—all scientific acceptances are provisional. However, Popper's theories were met by criticism, with opponents decrying the fact that such thinking leads to science based on hypotheses that are "the best of a bad lot."

Another aspect of science that was plumbed by philosophers was the role of explanation in scientific enterprises.

Some early 20th-century philosophers rejected the long-held belief that one of the aims of the natural sciences is to explain phenomena by noting that explanations are invariably subjective and that accurate predictions and the ability to control are all that is needed for "good science." This dismissal of explanation was countered by many prominent philosophers of science, most notably Hempel, who argued that explanations should not provide a feeling of "at homeness," since many advances in science produce feelings of unsettling newness. Instead, he posited that explanations are arguments that use laws of nature to show that phenomenon to be explained should have been expected. His approach, which came to be known as the covering-law model, ultimately proved to have many flaws, but his efforts to reground explanation as a central feature of science led later philosophers to build upon his work.

The issues of uncertainty that affected Hempel's work with explanation were echoed in investigations into scientific laws. The very act of using scientific laws as a basis of philosophical interest was questioned by scholars who argued that even certain groundbreaking scientific revelations that result in a wealth of subsequent findings—such as Watson and Crick's discovery of the molecular structure of DNA—do not produce any true new scientific laws. Similarly, the utility of scientific theories has been increasingly interrogated by contemporary scientific philosophers. The three major philosophic conceptions of theories were the axiomatic, the semantic, and the historicist, the latter of which was the creation of Thomas S. Kuhn, one of history's most influential philosophers of science. Kuhn's conception was put forth in his landmark book *The Structure of Scientific Revolutions* (1962), where he argued that philosophers should consider "paradigms" rather than theories. Kuhn's definition of a paradigm (which transcended philosophical circles to become a common feature in academic disciplines as far-ranging as literary theory and political science) took into account the entire program of research that comes out of a particular theory, since no scientific theory happens inside a vacuum, isolated from other work.

This focus on theories led some philosophers and scientists to speculate that there may be a single unifying theory that ties together all of the sciences. The origin of such thinking can be found in the reductive nature of many of the sciences. For example, social sciences can, in part, be based on the biological imperatives of humans. Human biology can be viewed as incredibly complex molecular reactions, and the chemistry of these reactions are based on the physics of the forming and breaking of chemical bonds. If a scholar were to be able to sort through and compress these dependencies, he or she could produce a catch-all "theory of everything."

The idea of a neat and tidy reductive theory was compelling to many, but in practice, attempts to boil down the complexities of the many sciences was doomed from the start. One of the harshest critics of such "vertical reduction" was Nancy Cartwright, who broadened her attack to also include "horizontal reduction," which is the concept that models and generalizations have expansive scope. She pointed out that, while there are many real-world instances where, say, Newton's second law can be readily applied to bodies in motion, there are numerous other situations where a body's trajectory cannot be predicted by Newtonian law (such as a dollar bill being dropped from a high window on a windy day). Cartwright noted that current scientific reasoning shows that the world is dappled with areas of model-able order and areas of disorder that inherently resist modeling, an argument that effectively shoots down any concept of scientific unity.

The majority of the topics discussed above hewed to the logical-empiricist point of view, which was the dominant school in the philosophy of science throughout the early 20th century. However, in the 1950s, a historicist viewpoint began to gain traction among scholars. Led by the work of Kuhn, N.R. Hanson, Stephen Toulmin, and Paul Feyerabend, the historicist critique focused on the insufficiencies of the logical-empiricist approach to the major developments in the history of science. The traditional view of science is that advances build upon each other over time and result in an accumulation of truth. Logical empiricists promoted a version of this outlook by stressing the "observation language" of scientific discoveries, meaning that which derives its meaning from direct experience. The historicist critique argued that throughout the history of science, "correct" outcomes were not always arrived at rationally while a number of the ultimately "incorrect" hypotheses were grounded in perfectly sound reasoning.

The leading figure in this approach was, once again, Thomas Kuhn. He proposed that scientific inquiries begin with a clash of various perspectives that, over time, resolve an issue and lead to the formation of a paradigm that investigators follow. The resulting pursuit of the paradigmatic finding creates a series of puzzles that researchers must solve. The failure to solve a puzzle does not, in Kuhn's view, mean that the paradigm is somehow incorrect but instead reflects bad research. If failed puzzles pile up over time and a rival viewpoint emerges, then the scientific community shifts its focus to the rival in what Kuhn characterized as a "revolution." His conception was that science consisted of a series of these revolutions where the old unsolvable puzzles are not to be thought of as "wrong" per se, but as simply unsuccessful pursuits that contain no value judgments. As a result, Kuhn's thinking upended traditional assumptions about scientific progress and rationality.

It was not just scientific progress that was placed under scrutiny by philosophers but also scientific realism. The concept of scientific realism began to be questioned in the wake of the logical-empiricist analyses of theories. Some logical empiricists felt that certain scientific terms that describe unobservable entities, such as *electron*, should only be treated as placeholders that allow scientists to make predictions about observables and not as definitive, "real" objects. An opposing realist view came to the forefront during the 1960s and '70s that is best exemplified by an argument from the philosopher Grover Maxwell. He noted that a large proportion of the populace are unable to observe much without first putting on corrective lenses, so where does one draw the line between observables and unobservables? If the line is so blurred, Maxwell posited, then all theoretically "real" objects should be treated as real since there is no hard-and-fast delineation. A cogent antirealist argument came to the fore in the 1990s, but, ultimately, the philosophical consensus has settled on what is known as "piecemeal realism," which claims that treating unobservables as being "literally so" is permissible, but that realism should hold sway in specific cases.

As the changing views of realism show, the philosophy of science rarely produces concrete findings from the start; the practice, like science itself, consists of a series of proposals and counterproposals that usually result in compromise. Despite the fact that the treatment of the field as a standalone academic discipline is a relatively new development, the firm roots of the field that were established by the likes of Carnap, Hempel, and Kuhn assure that the back-and-forth of the science of studying science will continue to thrive for the foreseeable future.

FROM NATURAL PHILOSOPHY TO THEORIES OF METHOD

The history of philosophy is intertwined with the history of the natural sciences. Long before the 19th century, when the term *science* began to be used with its modern meaning, those who are now counted among the major figures in the history of Western philosophy were often equally famous for their contributions to "natural philosophy," the bundle of inquiries now designated as sciences. Aristotle (384–322 BCE) was the first great biologist; René Descartes (1596–1650) formulated analytic geometry ("Cartesian geometry") and discovered the laws of the reflection and refraction of light; Gottfried Wilhelm Leibniz (1646–1716) laid claim to priority in the invention of the calculus; and Immanuel Kant (1724–1804) offered the basis of a still-current hypothesis regarding the formation of the solar system (the Kant-Laplace nebular hypothesis).

In reflecting on human knowledge, the great philosophers also offered accounts of the aims and methods of the sciences, ranging from Aristotle's studies in logic through the proposals of Francis Bacon (1561–1626) and Descartes, which were instrumental in shaping 17th-century science. They were joined in these reflections by the most eminent

Aristotle, marble portrait bust, Roman copy (2nd century BCE) of a Greek original (c. 325 BCE); in the Museo Nazionale Romano, Rome. A Dagli Orti/© DeA Picture Library

natural scientists. Galileo (1564–1642) supplemented his arguments about the motions of earthly and heavenly bodies with claims about the roles of mathematics and experiment in discovering facts about nature. Similarly, the account given by Isaac Newton (1642–1727) of his system of the natural world is punctuated by a defense of his methods and an outline of a positive program for scientific inquiry. Antoine-Laurent Lavoisier (1743–94), James Clerk Maxwell (1831–79), Charles Darwin (1809–82), and Albert Einstein (1879–1955) all continued this tradition, offering their own insights into the character of the scientific enterprise.

The two disciplines are so inexorably intertwined that it may sometimes be difficult to decide whether to classify an older figure as a philosopher or a scientist. In such an instance, the archaic "natural philosopher" may sometimes seem to provide a good compromise.

LOGICAL POSITIVISM AND LOGICAL EMPIRICISM

A series of developments in early 20th-century philosophy made the general philosophy of science central to philosophy in the English-speaking world. Inspired by the articulation of mathematical logic, or formal logic, in the work of the philosophers Gottlob Frege (1848–1925) and Bertrand Russell (1872–1970) and the mathematician David Hilbert (1862–1943), a group of European philosophers known as the Vienna Circle attempted to diagnose the difference between the inconclusive debates that mark the history of philosophy and the firm accomplishments of the sciences they admired. They offered criteria of meaningfulness, or "cognitive significance," aiming to demonstrate that traditional philosophical questions (and their proposed answers) are meaningless. The correct task of philosophy, they suggested, is to formulate a "logic of the sciences" that would be analogous to the logic of pure mathematics formulated by Frege, Russell, and Hilbert. In the light of logic, they thought, genuinely fruitful inquiries could be freed from the encumbrances of traditional philosophy.

Gottlob Frege. Courtesy of the Universitatsbibliothek, Jena, Ger.

THE VIENNA CIRCLE

In the 1920s, a group of philosophers, scientists, and mathematicians met regularly in Vienna to investigate scientific language and scientific methodology. The philosophical movement associated with the group, dubbed the Vienna Circle, has been called variously logical positivism, logical empiricism, scientific empiricism, neopositivism, and the unity of science movement.

The work of its members, although not unanimous in the treatment of many issues, was distinguished, first, by its attention to the form of scientific theories, in the belief that the logical structure of any particular scientific theory could be specified quite apart from its content. Second, they formulated a verifiability principle or criterion of meaning, a claim that the meaningfulness of a proposition is grounded in experience and observation. For this reason, the statements of ethics, metaphysics, religion, and aesthetics were held to be assertorically meaningless. Third, and as a result of the two other points, a doctrine of unified science was espoused. Thus, no fundamental differences were seen to exist between the physical and the biological sciences or between the natural and the social sciences.

The founder and leader of the group was Moritz Schlick, who was an epistemologist and philosopher of science. Among its members were Gustav Bergmann, Rudolf Carnap, Herbert Feigl, Philipp Frank, Kurt Gödel, Otto Neurath, and Friedrich Waismann; and among the members of a cognate group, the Gesellschaft fur empirische Philosophie ("Society for Empirical Philosophy"), which met in Berlin, were Carl Hempel and Hans Reichenbach. A formal declaration of the group's intentions was issued in 1929 with the publication of the manifesto *Wissenschaftliche Weltauffassung: Der Wiener Kreis* ("Scientific Conception of the World: The Vienna Circle"), and in that year the first in a series of congresses organized by the group took place in Prague. In 1938, with the onset of World War II, political pressure was brought to bear against the group, and it disbanded, many of its members fleeing to the United States and a few to Great Britain.

To carry through this bold program, a sharp criterion of meaningfulness was required. Unfortunately, as they tried to use the tools of mathematical logic to specify the criterion, the logical positivists (as they came to be known) encountered unexpected difficulties. Again and again, promising proposals were either so lax that they allowed the cloudiest pronouncements of traditional metaphysics to count as meaningful, or so restrictive that they excluded the most cherished hypotheses of the sciences. Faced with these discouraging results, logical positivism evolved into a more moderate movement, logical empiricism. (Many historians of philosophy treat this movement as a late version of logical positivism and accordingly do not refer to it by any distinct name.) Logical empiricists took as central the task of understanding the distinctive virtues of the natural sciences. In effect, they proposed that the search for a theory of scientific method—undertaken by Aristotle, Bacon, Descartes, and others—could be carried out more thoroughly with the tools of mathematical logic. Not only did they see a theory of scientific method as central to philosophy, but they also viewed that theory as valuable for aspiring areas of inquiry in which an explicit understanding of method might resolve debates and clear away confusions. Their agenda was deeply influential in subsequent philosophy of science.

LOGICS OF DISCOVERY AND JUSTIFICATION

An ideal theory of scientific method would consist of instructions that could lead an investigator from ignorance to knowledge. Descartes and Bacon sometimes wrote as if they could offer so ideal a theory, but after the mid-20th century the orthodox view was that this is too much to ask for. Following Hans Reichenbach (1891–1953), philosophers often distinguished between the "context of discovery" and the "context of justification." Once a hypothesis has been proposed, there are canons of logic that determine whether or not it should be accepted—that is, there are rules of method that hold in the context of justification. There are, however, no such rules that will guide someone to formulate the right hypothesis, or even hypotheses that are plausible or fruitful. The logical empiricists were led to this conclusion by reflecting on cases in which scientific discoveries were made either by imaginative leaps or by lucky accidents; a favourite example was the hypothesis by August Kekulé (1829–96) that benzene molecules have a hexagonal structure, allegedly formed as he was dozing in front of a fire in which the live coals seemed to resemble a snake devouring its own tail.

Although the idea that there cannot be a logic of scientific discovery often assumed the status of orthodoxy, it was not unquestioned. One of the implications of the influential work of Thomas Kuhn (1922–96) in the philosophy of science was that considerations of the likelihood of future discoveries of particular kinds are sometimes entangled with judgments of evidence, so discovery can be dismissed as an irrational process only if one is prepared to concede that the irrationality also infects the context of justification itself.

Sometimes in response to Kuhn and sometimes for independent reasons, philosophers tried to analyze particular instances of complex scientific discoveries, showing how the scientists involved appear to have followed identifiable methods and strategies. The most ambitious response to the empiricist orthodoxy tried to do exactly what was abandoned as hopeless—to wit, specify formal procedures for producing hypotheses in response to an available body of evidence. So, for example, the American philosopher Clark Glymour and his associates wrote computer programs to generate hypotheses in response to statistical evidence, hypotheses that often introduced new variables that did not themselves figure in the data. These programs were applied in various traditionally difficult areas of natural and social scientific research. Perhaps, then, logical empiricism was premature in writing off the context of discovery as beyond the range of philosophical analysis.

In contrast, logical empiricists worked vigorously on the problem of understanding scientific justification. Inspired by the thought that Frege, Russell, and Hilbert had given a completely precise specification of the conditions under which premises deductively imply a conclusion, philosophers of science hoped to offer a "logic of confirmation" that would identify, with equal precision, the conditions under which a body of evidence supported a scientific hypothesis. They recognized, of course, that a series of experimental reports on the expansion of metals under heat would not deductively imply the general conclusion that all metals expand when heated—for even if all the reports were correct, it would still be possible that the very next metal to be examined failed to expand under heat. Nonetheless, it seemed that a sufficiently large and sufficiently varied collection of reports would provide some support, even strong support, for the generalization. The philosophical task was to make precise this intuitive judgment about support.

During the 1940s, two prominent logical empiricists, Rudolf Carnap (1891–1970) and Carl Hempel (1905–97), made influential attempts to solve this problem. Carnap offered a valuable distinction between various versions of the question. The "qualitative" problem of confirmation seeks to specify the conditions under which a body of evidence E supports, to some degree, a hypothesis H. The "comparative" problem seeks to determine when one body of evidence E supports a hypothesis H more than a body of evidence E* supports a hypothesis H* (here E and E* might be the same, or H and H* might be the same). Finally, the "quantitative" problem seeks a function that assigns a numerical measure of the degree to which E supports H. The comparative problem attracted little attention, but Hempel attacked the qualitative problem while Carnap concentrated on the quantitative problem.

It would be natural to assume that the qualitative problem is the easier of the two, and even that it is quite straightforward. Many scientists (and philosophers) were attracted to the idea of hypothetico-deductivism, or the hypothetico-deductive method: scientific hypotheses are confirmed by deducing from them predictions about empirically determinable phenomena, and, when the predictions hold good, support accrues to the hypotheses from which those predictions derive. Hempel's explorations revealed why so simple a view could not be maintained. An apparently innocuous point about support seems to be that, if E confirms H, then E confirms any statement that can be deduced from H. Suppose, then, that H deductively implies E, and E has been ascertained by observation or experiment. If H is now conjoined with any arbitrary statement, the resulting conjunction will also deductively imply E. Hypothetico-deductivism says that this conjunction is confirmed by the evidence. By the innocuous point, E confirms any deductive consequence of the conjunction. One such deductive consequence is the arbitrary statement. So one reaches the conclusion that E, which might be anything whatsoever, confirms any arbitrary statement.

Rudolf Carnap, 1960. **Courtesy of the University of California, Los Angeles**

To see how bad this is, consider one of the great predictive theories—for example, Newton's account of the motions of the heavenly bodies. Hypothetico-deductivism looks promising in cases like this, precisely because Newton's theory seems to yield many predictions that can be checked and found to be correct. But if one tacks on to Newtonian theory any doctrine one pleases—perhaps the claim that global warming is the result of the activities of elves at the North Pole—then the expanded theory will equally yield the old predictions. On the account of confirmation just offered, the predictions confirm the

THE HYPOTHETICO-DEDUCTIVE METHOD

Also called H-D method or simply H-D, the hypothetico-deductive method is a procedure for the construction of a scientific theory that will account for results obtained through direct observation and experimentation and that will, through inference, predict further effects that can then be verified or disproved by empirical evidence derived from other experiments.

An early version of the hypothetico-deductive method was proposed by the Dutch physicist Christiaan Huygens (1629–95). The method generally assumes that properly formed theories are conjectures intended to explain a set of observable data. These hypotheses, however, cannot be conclusively established until the consequences that logically follow from them are verified through additional observations and experiments. The method treats theory as a deductive system in which particular empirical phenomena are explained by relating them back to general principles and definitions. However, it rejects the claim of Caresian mechanics that those principles and definitions are self-evident and valid; it assumes that their validity is determined only by the exact light their consequences throw on previously unexplained phenomena or on actual scientific problems.

expanded theory and any statement that follows deductively from it, including the elfin warming theory.

Hempel's work showed that this was only the start of the complexities of the problem of qualitative confirmation, and, although he and later philosophers made headway in addressing the difficulties, it seemed to many confirmation theorists that the quantitative problem was more tractable. Carnap's own attempts to tackle that problem, carried out in the 1940s and '50s, aimed to emulate the achievements of deductive logic. Carnap considered artificial systems whose expressive power falls dramatically short of the languages actually used in the practice of the sciences, and he hoped to define for any pair of statements in his restricted languages a function that would measure the degree to which the second supports the first. His painstaking research made it apparent that there were infinitely many functions (indeed, continuum many—a "larger" infinity corresponding to the size of the set of real numbers) satisfying the criteria he considered admissible. Despite the failure of the official project, however, he argued in detail for a connection between confirmation and probability, showing that, given certain apparently reasonable assumptions, the degree-of-confirmation function must satisfy the axioms of the probability calculus.

BAYESIAN CONFIRMATION

That conclusion was extended in the most prominent contemporary approach to issues of confirmation, so-called Bayesianism, named for the English clergyman and mathematician Thomas Bayes (1702–61). The guiding thought of Bayesianism is that acquiring evidence modifies the probability rationally assigned to a hypothesis.

For a simple version of the thought, a hackneyed example will suffice. If one is asked what probability should be assigned to drawing the king of hearts from a standard deck of 52 cards, one would almost certainly answer $\frac{1}{52}$. Suppose now that one obtains information to the effect that a face card (ace, king, queen, or jack) will be drawn; now the probability shifts from $\frac{1}{52}$ to $\frac{1}{16}$. If one learns that the card will be red, the probability increases to $\frac{1}{8}$. Adding the information that the card is neither an ace nor a queen makes the probability $\frac{1}{4}$. As the evidence comes in, one forms a probability that is conditional on the information one now has, and in this case the evidence drives the probability upward. (This need not have been the case: if one had learned that the card drawn was a jack, the probability of drawing the king of hearts would have plummeted to 0.)

Bayes is renowned for a theorem that explains an important relationship between conditional probabilities. If, at a particular stage in an inquiry, a scientist assigns a probability to the hypothesis H, $Pr(H)$—call this the prior probability of H—and assigns probabilities to the evidential reports conditionally on the truth of H, $Pr_H(E)$, and conditionally on the falsehood of H, $Pr_{-H}(E)$, Bayes's theorem gives a value for the probability of the hypothesis H conditionally on the evidence E by the formula

$$Pr_E(H) = {}^{Pr(H)Pr_H(E)}\!/\!_{[Pr(H)Pr_H(E) + Pr(-H)Pr_{-H}(E)]}$$

One of the attractive features of this approach to confirmation is that when the evidence would be highly improbable if the hypothesis were false—that is, when $Pr_{-H}(E)$ is extremely small—it is easy to see how a hypothesis with a quite low prior probability can acquire a probability close to 1 when the evidence comes in. (This holds even when $Pr(H)$ is quite small and $Pr(-H)$, the

Deducing the likelihood that a particular card will be drawn from a full deck of cards based on mounting evidence is a simple example of Bayesianism in action. **Payless Images /Shutterstock.com**

probability that H is false, correspondingly large; if E follows deductively from H, $Pr_H(E)$ will be 1; hence, if $Pr_{-H}(E)$ is tiny, the numerator of the right side of the formula will be very close to the denominator, and the value of the right side thus approaches 1.)

Any use of Bayes's theorem to reconstruct scientific reasoning plainly depends on the idea that scientists can assign the pertinent probabilities, both the prior probabilities and the probabilities of the evidence conditional on various hypotheses. But how should scientists conclude that the probability of an interesting hypothesis takes on a particular value or that a certain evidential finding would be extremely improbable if the interesting hypothesis were false? The simple example about drawing from a deck of cards is potentially misleading in this respect, because in this case there seems to be available a straightforward means of calculating the probability that a specific card, such as the king of hearts, will be drawn. There is no obvious analogue with respect to scientific hypotheses. It would seem foolish, for example, to suppose that there is some list of potential scientific hypotheses, each of which is equally likely to hold true of the universe.

Bayesians are divided in their responses to this difficulty. A relatively small minority—the so-called "objective" Bayesians—hope to find objective criteria for the rational assignment of prior probabilities. The majority position—"subjective" Bayesianism, sometimes also called personalism—supposes, by contrast, that no such criteria are to be found. The only limits on rational choice of prior probabilities stem from the need to give each truth of logic and mathematics the probability 1 and to provide a value different from both 0 and 1 for every empirical statement. The former proviso reflects the view that the laws of logic and mathematics cannot be false; the latter embodies the idea that any statement whose truth or falsity is not determined by the laws of logic and mathematics might turn out to be true (or false).

On the face of it, subjective Bayesianism appears incapable of providing any serious reconstruction of scientific reasoning. Thus, imagine two scientists of the late 17th century who differ in their initial assessments of Newton's account of the motions of the heavenly bodies. One begins by assigning the Newtonian hypothesis a small but significant probability; the other attributes a probability that is truly minute. As they collect evidence, both modify their probability judgments in accordance with Bayes's theorem, and, in both instances, the probability of the Newtonian hypothesis goes up. For the first scientist it approaches 1. The second, however, has begun with so minute a probability that, even with a large body of positive evidence for the Newtonian hypothesis, the final value assigned is still tiny. From the subjective Bayesian perspective, both have proceeded impeccably. Yet, at the end of the day, they diverge quite radically in their assessment of the hypothesis.

If one supposes that the evidence obtained is like that acquired in the decades after the publication of Newton's hypothesis in his *Principia (Philosophiae naturalis principia mathematica*, 1687), it may seem possible to resolve the issue as follows: even though both investigators were initially skeptical (both assigned small prior probabilities to Newton's hypothesis), one gave the hypothesis a serious chance and the other did not; the inquirer who started with the truly minute probability made an irrational judgment that infects the conclusion. No subjective Bayesian can tolerate this diagnosis, however. The Newtonian hypothesis is not a logical or mathematical truth (or a logical or mathematical falsehood), and both scientists give it a probability different from 0 and 1. By subjective Bayesian standards, that is all rational inquirers are asked to do.

The orthodox response to worries of this type is to offer mathematical theorems that demonstrate how individuals starting with different prior probabilities will eventually converge on a common value. Indeed, were the imaginary investigators to keep going long enough, their eventual assignments of probability would differ by an amount as tiny as one cared to make it. In the long run, scientists who lived by Bayesian standards would agree. But, as the English economist (and contributor to the theory of probability and confirmation) John Maynard Keynes (1883–1946) once observed, "in the long run we are all dead." Scientific decisions are inevitably made in a finite period of time, and the same mathematical explorations that yield convergence theorems will also show that, given a fixed period for decision making, however long it may be, there can be people who satisfy the subjective Bayesian requirements and yet remain about as far apart as possible, even at the end of the evidence-gathering period.

ELIMINATIVISM AND FALSIFICATION

Subjective Bayesianism is currently the most popular view of the confirmation of scientific hypotheses, partly because it seems to accord with important features of confirmation and partly because it is both systematic and precise. But the worry just outlined is not the only concern that critics press and defenders endeavour to meet. Among others is the objection that explicit assignments of probabilities seem to figure in scientific reasoning only when the focus is on statistical hypotheses. A more homely view of testing and the appraisal of hypotheses suggests that scientists proceed by the method of Sherlock Holmes: they formulate rival hypotheses and apply tests designed to eliminate some until the hypothesis that remains, however antecedently implausible, is judged correct. Unlike Bayesianism, this approach to scientific reasoning is explicitly concerned with the acceptance and rejection of hypotheses and thus seems far closer to the everyday practice of scientists than the revision of probabilities. But eliminativism, as this view is sometimes called, also faces serious challenges.

The first main worry centres on the choice of alternatives. In the setting of the country-house murder, Sherlock Holmes (or his counterpart) has a clear list of suspects. In scientific inquiries, however, no such complete roster of potential hypotheses is available. For all anyone knows, the correct hypothesis might not figure among the rivals under consideration. How then can the eliminative procedure provide any confidence in the hypothesis left standing at the end? Eliminativists are forced to concede that this is a genuine difficulty and that there can be many situations in which it is appropriate to wonder whether the initial construction of possibilities was unimaginative. If they believe that inquirers are sometimes justified in accepting the hypothesis that survives an eliminative process, then they must formulate criteria for distinguishing such situations. By the early 21st century, no one had yet offered any such precise criteria.

An apparent method of avoiding the difficulty just raised would be to emphasize the tentative character of scientific judgment. This tactic was pursued with considerable thoroughness by the Austrian-born British

Eliminativism is a form of scientific inquiry in which various hypotheses are tested by an investigation of the evidence at hand, and the least probable eliminated. iStockphoto/Thinkstock

philosopher Karl Popper (1902–92), whose views about scientific reasoning probably had more influence on practicing scientists than those of any other philosopher. Although not himself a logical positivist, Popper shared many of the aspirations of those who wished to promote "scientific philosophy." Instead of supposing that traditional philosophical discussions failed because they lapsed into meaninglessness, he offered a criterion of demarcation in terms of the falsifiability of genuine scientific hypotheses. That criterion was linked to his reconstruction of scientific reasoning: science, he claimed, consists of bold conjectures that scientists endeavour to refute, and the conjectures that survive are given tentative acceptance. Popper thus envisaged an eliminative process that begins with the rival hypotheses that a particular group of scientists happen to have thought of, and he responded to the worry that the successful survival of a series of tests might not be any indicator of truth by emphasizing that scientific acceptance is always tentative and provisional.

Popper's influence on scientists reflected his ability to capture features that investigators recognized in their own reasoning. Philosophers, however, were less convinced. For however much he emphasized the tentative character of acceptance, Popper—like the scientists who read him—plainly thought that surviving the eliminative process makes a hypothesis more worthy of being pursued or applied in a practical context. The "conjectures" are written into textbooks, taught to aspiring scientists, relied on in further research, and used as the basis for interventions in nature that sometimes affect the well-being of large numbers of people. If they attain some privileged status by enduring the fire of eliminative testing, then Popper's view covertly presupposes a solution to the worry that elimination has merely isolated the best of a bad lot. If, on the other hand, the talk about "tentative acceptance" is taken seriously, and survival confers no special privilege, then it is quite mysterious why anybody should be entitled to use the science "in the books" in the highly consequential ways it is in fact used. Popper's program was attractive because it embraced the virtues of eliminativism, but the rhetoric of "bold conjectures" and "tentative acceptance" should be viewed as a way of ducking a fundamental problem that eliminativists face.

A second major worry about eliminativism charged that the notion of falsification is more complex than eliminativists (including Popper) allowed. As the philosopher-physicist Pierre Duhem (1861–1916) pointed out, experiments and observations typically test a bundle of different hypotheses. When a complicated experiment reveals results that are dramatically at odds with predictions, a scientist's first thought is not to abandon a cherished hypothesis but to check whether the apparatus is working properly, whether the samples used are pure, and so forth. A particularly striking example of this situation comes from the early responses to the Copernican system. Astronomers of the late 16th century, virtually all of whom believed in the traditional view that the heavenly bodies revolved around the Earth, pointed out that if, as Copernicus claimed, the Earth is in motion, then the stars should be seen at different angles at different times of the year; but no differences were observed, and thus Copernicanism, they concluded, is false. Galileo, a champion of the Copernican view, replied that the argument is fallacious. The apparent constancy of the angles at which the stars are seen is in conflict not with Copernicanism alone but with the joint hypothesis that the Earth moves and that the stars are relatively close. Galileo proposed to "save" Copernicanism from falsification by abandoning the latter part of the hypothesis, claiming instead that the universe is much larger than had been suspected and that the nearest stars are so distant that the differences in their angular positions cannot be detected with the naked eye. (He was vindicated in the 19th century, when improved telescopes revealed the stellar parallax.)

Eliminativism needs an account of when it is rationally acceptable to divert an experimental challenge to some auxiliary hypothesis and when the hypothesis under test should be abandoned. It must distinguish the case of Galileo from that of someone who insists on a pet hypothesis in the teeth of the evidence, citing the possibility that hitherto unsuspected spirits are disrupting the trials. The problem is especially severe for Popper's version of eliminativism, since, if all hypotheses are tentative, there would appear to be no recourse to background knowledge, on the basis of which some possibilities can be dismissed as just not serious.

UNDERDETERMINATION

The complexities of the notion of falsification, originally diagnosed by Duhem, had considerable impact on contemporary philosophy of science through the work of the American philosopher W.V.O. Quine (1908–2000). Quine proposed a general thesis of the underdetermination of theory by evidence, arguing that it is always possible to preserve any hypothesis in the face of any evidence. This thesis can be understood as a bare logical point, to the effect that an investigator can always find some consistent way of dealing with observations or experiments so as to continue to maintain a chosen hypothesis (perhaps by claiming that the apparent observations are the result of hallucination). So conceived, it appears trivial. Alternatively, one can interpret it as proposing that all the criteria of rationality and scientific method permit some means of protecting the favoured hypothesis from the apparently refuting results. On the latter reading, Quine went considerably beyond Duhem, who held that the "good sense" of scientists enables them to distinguish legitimate from illegitimate ways of responding to recalcitrant findings.

The stronger interpretation of the thesis is sometimes inspired by a small number of famous examples from the history of physics. In the early 18th century, there was a celebrated debate between Leibniz and Samuel Clarke (1675–1729), an acolyte of Newton, over the "true motions" of the heavenly bodies. Clarke, following Newton, defined true motion as motion with respect to absolute space and claimed that the centre of mass of the solar system was at rest with respect to absolute space. Leibniz countered by suggesting that, if the centre of mass of the solar system were moving with uniform velocity with respect to absolute space, all the observations one could ever make would be the same as they would be if the universe were displaced in absolute space. In effect, he offered infinitely many alternatives to the Newtonian theory, each of which seemed equally well supported by any data that could be collected. Recent discussions in the foundations of physics sometimes suggested a similar moral. Perhaps there are rival versions of string theory, each of which is equally well supported by all the evidence that could become available.

Such examples, which illustrate the complexities inherent in the notion of falsification, raise two important questions: first, when cases of underdetermination arise, what is it reasonable to believe? And second, how frequently do such cases arise? One very natural response to the motivating examples from physics is to suggest that, when one recognizes that genuinely rival hypotheses could each be embedded in a body of theory that would be equally well supported by any available evidence, one should look for a more minimal hypothesis that will somehow "capture what is common" to the apparent alternatives. If that natural response is right, then the examples do not really support Quine's sweeping thesis, for they do not permit the rationality of believing either (or any) of a pair (or collection) of alternatives but rather insist on articulating a different, more minimal, view.

A second objection to the strong thesis of underdetermination is that the historical examples are exceptional. Certain kinds of mathematical theories, together with plausible assumptions about the evidence that can be collected, allow for the formulation of serious alternatives. In

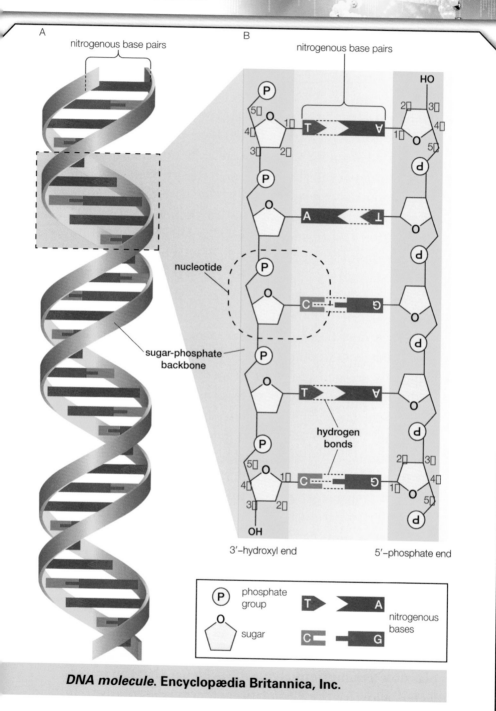

DNA molecule. Encyclopædia Britannica, Inc.

most areas of science, however, there is no obvious way to invoke genuine rivals. Since the 1950s, for example, scientists have held that DNA molecules have the structure of a double helix, in which the bases jut inward, like the rungs of a ladder, and that there are simple rules of base pairing. If Quine's global thesis were correct, there should be some scientific rival that would account equally well for the vast range of data that supports this hypothesis. Not only has no such rival been proposed, but there are simply no good reasons for thinking that any exists.

Many contemporary discussions in the philosophy of science seek algorithms for scientific discovery, attempt to respond to the worries about Bayesian confirmation theory or to develop a rival, and explore the notions of falsification and underdetermination. These discussions often continue the inquiries begun by the principal logical empiricists—Carnap, Hempel, Reichenbach, and Popper—adhering to the conceptions of science and philosophy that were central to their enterprise. For a significant number of philosophers, however, these discussions have been transformed by reactions to logical empiricism, the historicist turn in the philosophy of science, and the increasing interest in the social dimensions of scientific research.

CHAPTER 2

EXPLANATIONS, LAWS, AND THEORIES

The logical-empiricist project of contrasting the virtues of science with the defects of other human ventures was only partly carried out by attempting to understand the logic of scientific justification. In addition, empiricists hoped to analyze the forms of scientific knowledge. They saw the sciences as arriving at laws of nature that were systematically assembled into theories. Laws and theories were valuable not only for providing bases for prediction and intervention but also for yielding explanation of natural phenomena. In some discussions, philosophers also envisaged an ultimate aim for the systematic and explanatory work of the sciences: the construction of a unified science in which nature was understood in maximum depth.

EXPLANATION AS DEDUCTION

The idea that the aims of the natural sciences are explanation, prediction, and control dates back at least to the 19th

UNIFIED SCIENCE

In the philosophy of logical positivism, unified science is a doctrine holding that all sciences share the same language, laws, and method or at least one or two of these features. A unity-of-science movement arose in the Vienna Circle, a group of scientists and philosophers that met regularly in Vienna in the 1920s and '30s and was associated in particular with Rudolf Carnap and Otto Neurath. Versions of the unity-of-science thesis are still supported by many contemporary philosophers of science.

The claim that all sciences share a common language may mean one of two things. First, for the logical positivist, the claim often meant that all scientific terms could be restated as, or reduced to, a set of basic statements, or "protocol" sentences, describing immediate experience or perception. Second, more recently, unity of language has meant the reduction of all scientific terms to terms of physics.

Otto Neurath, one of the proponents of the unity of science movement espoused by members of the Vienna Circle. Imagno/ Hulton Archive/Getty Images

The unity of law means that the laws of the various sciences are to be deduced from some set of fundamental laws, often thought to be those of physics.

Finally, the unity of method means that the procedures for testing and supporting statements in the various sciences are basically the same. The procedures of the populations biologist, for example, purportedly are fundamentally no different than those of the theoretical physicist.

century. Early in the 20th century, however, some prominent scholars of science were inclined to dismiss the ideal of explanation, contending that explanation is inevitably a subjective matter. Explanation, it was suggested, is a matter of feeling "at home" with the phenomena, and good science need provide nothing of the sort. It is enough if it achieves accurate predictions and an ability to control.

THE WORK OF CARL HEMPEL

During the 1930s and '40s, philosophers fought back against this dismissal of explanation. Popper, Hempel, and Ernest Nagel (1901–85) all proposed an ideal of objective explanation and argued that explanation should be restored as one of the aims of the sciences. Their writings recapitulated in more precise form a view that had surfaced in earlier reflections on science from Aristotle onward. Hempel's formulations were the most detailed and systematic and the most influential.

Hempel explicitly conceded that many scientific advances fail to make one feel at home with the phenomena— and, indeed, that they sometimes replace a familiar world with something much stranger. He denied, however, that providing an explanation should yield any sense of "at homeness." First, explanations should give grounds for expecting the phenomenon to be explained, so that one no longer wonders why it came about but sees that it should have been anticipated; second, explanations should do this by making apparent how the phenomenon exemplifies the laws of nature. So, according to Hempel, explanations are arguments. The conclusion of the argument is a statement describing the phenomenon to be explained. The premises must include at least one law of nature and must provide support for the conclusion.

The simplest type of explanation is that in which the conclusion describes a fact or event and the premises provide deductive grounds for it. Hempel's celebrated example involved the cracking of a car radiator on a cold night. Here the conclusion to be explained might be formulated as the statement, "The radiator cracked on the night of January 10th." Among the premises would be statements describing the conditions ("The temperature on the night of January 10th fell to -10°C," etc.), as well as laws about the freezing of water, the pressure exerted by ice, and so forth. The premises would consitute an explanation because the conclusion follows from them deductively.

Hempel allowed for other forms of explanation—cases in which one deduces a law of nature from more general laws, as well as cases in which statistical laws are invoked to assign a high probability to the conclusion.

A statement that a car radiator had cracked on a midwinter's night is the classic example used by Carl Hempel to explain his brand of deductive reasoning. **Jeff Hutchens/ Photonica World/Getty Images**

Conforming to his main proposal that explanation consists in using the laws of nature to demonstrate that the phenomenon to be explained was to be expected, he insisted that every genuine explanation must appeal to some law (completely general or statistical) and that the premises must support the conclusion (either deductively or by conferring high probability). His models of explanation were widely accepted among philosophers for about 20 years, and they were welcomed by many investigators in the social sciences. During subsequent decades, however, they encountered severe criticism.

DIFFICULTIES

One obvious line of objection is that explanations, in ordinary life as well as in the sciences, rarely take the form of complete arguments. A clumsy person, for example, may explain why there is a stain on the carpet by confessing that he spilled the coffee, and a geneticist may account for an unusual fruit fly by claiming that there was a recombination of the parental genotypes. Hempel responded to this criticism by distinguishing between what is actually presented to someone who requests an explanation (the "explanation sketch") and the full objective explanation. A reply to an explanation seeker works because the explanation sketch can be combined with information that the person already possesses to enable him to arrive at the full explanation. The explanation sketch gains its explanatory force from the full explanation and contains the part of the full explanation that the questioner needs to know.

A second difficulty for Hempel's account resulted from his candid admission that he was unable to offer a full analysis of the notion of a scientific law. Laws are generalizations about a range of natural phenomena, sometimes universal ("Any two bodies attract one another with a force that is proportional to the product of their masses and inversely as the square of the distance between them") and sometimes statistical ("The chance that any particular allele will be transmitted to a gamete in meiosis is 50 percent"). Not every generalization, however, counts as a scientific law. There are streets on which every house is made of brick, but no judgment of the form "All houses on X street are made of brick" qualifies as a scientific law. As Reichenbach pointed out, there are accidental generalizations that seem to have very broad scope. Whereas the statement "All uranium spheres have a radius of less than one kilometre" is a matter of natural law (large uranium spheres would be unstable because of fundamental physical properties), the statement "All gold spheres have a radius of less than one kilometre" merely expresses a cosmic accident.

Intuitively, laws of nature seem to embody a kind of necessity: they do not simply describe the way that things happen to be, but, in some sense, they describe how things have to be. If one attempted to build a very large uranium sphere, one would be bound to fail. The prevalent attitude of logical empiricism, following the celebrated discussion of "necessary connections" in nature by the Scottish philosopher David Hume (1711–76), was to be wary of invoking notions of necessity. To be sure, logical empiricists recognized the necessity of logic and mathematics, but the laws of nature could hardly be conceived as necessary in this sense, for it is logically (and mathematically) possible that the universe had different laws. Indeed, one main hope of Hempel and his colleagues was to avoid difficulties with necessity by relying on the concepts of law and explanation. To say that there is a necessary connection between two types of events is, they proposed, simply to assert a lawlike succession—events of the first type are regularly succeeded by events of the second, and the succession is a matter of natural law. For this program to succeed, however, logical empiricism required an analysis of the notion of a law of nature that did not rely on the concept of necessity. Logical empiricists were admirably clear about what they wanted and about what had to be done to achieve it, but the project of providing the

David Hume, oil painting by Allan Ramsay, 1766. **Courtesy of the Scottish National Portrait Gallery**

pertinent analysis of laws of nature remained an open problem for them.

Scruples about necessary connections also generated a third class of difficulties for Hempel's project. There are examples of arguments that fit the patterns approved by Hempel and yet fail to count as explanatory, at least by ordinary lights. Imagine a flagpole that casts a shadow on the ground. One can explain the length of the shadow by deducing it (using trigonometry) from the height of the pole, the angle of elevation of the Sun, and the law of light propagation (i.e., the law that light travels in straight lines). So far this is unproblematic, for the little argument just outlined accords with Hempel's model of explanation. Notice, however, that there is a simple way to switch one of the premises with the conclusion: if one starts with the length of the shadow, the angle of elevation of the Sun, and the law of light propagation, one can deduce (using trigonometry) the height of the pole. The new derivation also accords with Hempel's model. But this is perturbing, because, while one thinks of the height of a pole as explaining the length of a shadow, one does not think of the length of a shadow as explaining the height of a pole. Intuitively, the amended derivation gets things backward, reversing the proper order of dependence. Given the commitments of logical empiricism, however, these diagnoses make no sense, and the two arguments are on a par with respect to explanatory power.

Although Hempel was sometimes inclined to "bite the bullet" and defend the explanatory worth of both arguments, most philosophers concluded that something was lacking. Furthermore, it seemed obvious what the missing ingredient was: shadows are causally dependent on poles in a way in which poles are not causally dependent on shadows. Since explanation must respect dependencies, the amended derivation is explanatorily worthless. Like the concept of natural necessity, however, the notion of causal dependence was anathema to logical empiricists—both had been targets of Hume's famous critique. To develop a satisfactory account of explanatory asymmetry, therefore, the logical empiricists needed to capture the idea of causal dependence by formulating conditions on genuine explanation in an acceptable idiom. Here too Hempel's program proved unsuccessful.

The fourth and last area in which trouble surfaced was in the treatment of probabilistic explanation. The probability ascribed to an outcome may vary, even quite dramatically, when new information is added. Hempel appreciated the point, recognizing that some statistical arguments that satisfy his conditions on explanation have the property that, even though all the premises are true, the support they lend to the conclusion would be radically undermined by adding extra premises. He attempted to solve the problem by adding further requirements. It was shown, however, that the new conditions were either ineffective or else trivialized the activity of probabilistic explanation.

Nor is it obvious that the fundamental idea of explaining through making the phenomena expectable can be sustained. To cite a famous example, one can explain the fact that the mayor contracted paresis by pointing out that he had previously had untreated syphilis, even though only 8 to 10 percent of people with untreated syphilis go on to develop paresis. In this instance, there is no statistical argument that confers high probability on the conclusion that the mayor contracted paresis—that conclusion remains improbable in light of the information advanced (85 percent of those with untreated syphilis do not get paresis). What seems crucial is the increase in probability, the fact that the probability of the conclusion rose from truly minute (paresis is extremely rare in the general population) to significant.

OTHER APPROACHES TO EXPLANATION

By the early 1970s, Hempel's approach to explanation (known as the covering-law model) seemed to be in trouble on a number of fronts, leading philosophers to canvass alternative treatments. An influential early proposal elaborated on the diagnosis of the last paragraph. Wesley Salmon (1925–2001) argued that probabilistic explanation should be taken as primary and that probabilistic explanations proceed by advancing information that raises the probability of the event (or fact) to be explained. Building on insights of Reichenbach, Salmon noted that there are cases in which giving information that raises probability is not explanatory: the probability that there is a storm goes up when one is told that the barometer is falling, but the fall of the barometer does not explain the occurrence of the storm. Reichenbach had analyzed such examples by seeing both the barometer's fall and the storm as effects of a common cause and offering a statistical condition to encompass situations in which common causes are present. Salmon extended Reichenbach's approach, effectively thinking of explanation as identifying the causes of phenomena and, consonant with empiricist scruples, attempting to provide an analysis of causation in terms of statistical relations. Unfortunately, it proved very difficult to reconstruct causal notions in statistical terms, and by the 1980s most philosophers had abandoned the attempt as hopeless.

Many, however—including Salmon—remained convinced that the notion of causation is central to the understanding of explanation and that scientific explanation is a matter of tracing causes. They were divided (and continue to be divided) into two groups: those who believed that Humean worries about causation are important and that, in consequence, a prior analysis of causation is needed, and those who think that Hume and his successors adopted a faulty picture of human knowledge, failing to recognize that people are capable of detecting causal relations perceptually. Salmon was the most prominent member of the first group, offering an intricate account of causal processes, causal propagation, and causal interaction by appealing (in later work) to the conservation of physical quantities. He also argued, against his earlier view, that causal explanation can sometimes proceed by making the event explained appear less probable than it formerly seemed. (Imagine a golfer whose ball strikes a tree and is deflected into the hole; a description of the initial trajectory of the ball would decrease the probability that the result will be a hole in one.)

Although regarding explanation as a matter of tracing causes responds in a very direct way to several of the problems encountered by Hempel's approach, it was not the only program in the recent theory of explanation. Some philosophers attempted to remain closer to Hempel's project by thinking of explanation in terms of unification. Especially concerned with examples of theoretical explanation in the sciences, they proposed that the hallmark of explanation is the ability to treat from a single perspective phenomena previously seen as highly disparate. They elaborate on the remark of the English biologist T.H. Huxley (1825–95) that "in the end, all phenomena are incomprehensible and that the task of science is to reduce the fundamental incomprehensibilities to the smallest possible number." This view, however, faced considerable technical difficulties in addressing some of the problems that arose for Hempel's approach. Its principal merits lay in the avoidance of any reliance on causal concepts and in the ability to give an account of explanation in areas of theoretical science in which talk of causation seems strained.

A different strategy began by questioning the Hempelian proposal that ordinary explanations consist in explanation sketches whose force derives from an unarticulated ideal explanation. Philosophers such as Peter Achinstein and Bas van Fraassen offered pragmatic theories, according to which what counts as an explanation is contextually determined. Their accounts remained close to the everyday practice of explaining, but, to the extent that they eschewed context-independent conditions on explanation, they encouraged a return to the idea that explanation is a purely subjective business, a matter of what an audience will be satisfied with. Indeed, van Fraassen welcomed a conclusion of this type, holding that explanatory power is not an objective virtue of scientific theories.

The current state of scientific explanation is thus highly fragmentary. Although many philosophers hold that explanations trace causes, there is still considerable disagreement about whether or not the notion of causation should be analyzed and, if so, how. The question of whether theoretical explanation can always be construed in causal terms remains open. It is unclear whether unifying the phenomena is an explanatory virtue and how a satisfactory notion of unification should be understood. Perhaps most fundamentally, there are controversies about whether there is a single notion of explanation that applies to all sciences, all contexts, and all periods and about whether explanatory power counts as an objective quality of theories.

SCIENTIFIC LAWS

Similar uncertainties affect recent discussions of scientific laws. As already noted, logical empiricism faced a difficult problem in distinguishing between genuine laws and accidental generalizations. Just as theorists of explanation sometimes liberated themselves from hard problems by invoking a concept hitherto held as taboo—the notion of causation—so too some philosophers championed an idea of natural necessity and tried to characterize it as precisely as possible. Others, more sympathetic to Hume's suspicions, continued the logical-empiricist project of analyzing the notion independently of the concept of natural necessity. The most important approach along these lines identifies the laws of nature as the generalizations that would figure in the best systematization of all natural phenomena. This suggestion fits naturally with the unificationist approach to explanation but encounters similar difficulties in articulating the idea of a "best systematization." Perhaps more fundamentally, it is not obvious that the concept of "all natural phenomena" is coherent (or, even if it is, whether this is something in which science should be interested).

There is an even more basic issue. Why is the notion of a scientific law of any philosophical interest? Within the framework of logical empiricism, and specifically within Hempel's approach to explanation, there was a clear answer. Explanations depend on laws, and the notion of law is to be explicated without appeal to suspect notions such as natural necessity. But Hempel's approach is now defunct, and many contemporary philosophers are suspicious of the old suspicions, prepared to be more tolerant of appeals to causation and natural necessity. What function, then, would an account of laws now serve?

James D. Watson, examining a model of deoxyriboneuclic acid (DNA). Along with Francis Crick, Watson won the Nobel Prize in Medicine for unraveling the molecular structure of DNA. Andreas Feininger/Time & Life Pictures/Getty Images

Perhaps the thought is that the search for the laws of nature is central to the scientific enterprise. But, to begin with, the scientific habit of labeling certain statements as "laws" seems extremely haphazard. There are areas, moreover, in which it is hard to find any laws—large tracts of the life and earth sciences, for example—and yet scientists in these areas are credited with the most important discoveries. James Watson 1928—and Francis Crick (1916–2004) won a Nobel Prize for one of the greatest scientific achievements of the 20th century (indeed, arguably the most fruitful), but it would be hard to state the law that they discovered. Accordingly, philosophers of science are beginning to abandon the notion that laws are central to

Francis Crick, whose work with James Watson on the structure of DNA, while a crucial game changer, could not be distilled into a scientific law. Oxford Science Archive/ Heritage-Images

science, focusing instead on the search for symmetries in physics, on the differing uses of approximate generalizations in biology, and on the deployment of models in numerous areas of the sciences.

SCIENTIFIC THEORIES

In addition to a general softening of the necessity of scientific laws, contemporary philosophy of science is moving beyond the question of the structure of scientific theories. For a variety of reasons, that question was of enormous importance to the logical positivists and to the logical empiricists. Mathematical logic supplied a clear conception: a theory is a collection of statements (the axioms of the theory) and their deductive consequences. The logical positivists showed how this conception could be applied in scientific cases—one could axiomatize the theory of relativity, for example.

THE AXIOMATIC CONCEPTION

The work of axiomatization was not an idle exercise, for the difficulties of formulating a precise criterion of cognitive significance (intended to separate good science from meaningless philosophical discussion) raised questions about the legitimacy of the special vocabulary that figures in scientific theories. Convinced that the sound and fury of German metaphysics—references to "Absolute Spirit" by Georg Wilhelm Friedrich Hegel (1770–1831) and talk of "the Nothing" by Martin Heidegger (1889–1976)— signified, indeed, nothing, logical positivists (and logical empiricists) recognized that they needed to show how terms such as *electron* and *covalent bond* were different.

They began from a distinction between two types of language. Observational language comprises all the terms that can be acquired by presentation of observable samples. Although they were skeptical about mixing psychology and philosophy, logical empiricists tacitly adopted a simple theory of learning: children can learn terms such as *red* by being shown appropriate swatches, *hot* by holding their hands under the right taps, and so forth. Logical empiricists denied that this observational vocabulary would suffice to define the special terms of theoretical science, the theoretical language that seemed to pick out unobservable entities and properties. Conceiving of theories as axiomatic systems, however, they drew a distinction between two types of axioms. Some axioms contain only theoretical vocabulary, while others contain both theoretical and observational terms. The latter, variously characterized as "correspondence rules" or "coordinating definitions," relate the theoretical and observational vocabularies, and it is through them that theoretical terms acquire what meaning they have.

The last formulation blurs an important difference between two schools within logical empiricism. According to one school, the theoretical terms are "partially interpreted" by the correspondence rules, so, for example, if one such rule is that an electron produces a particular kind of track in a cloud chamber, then many possibilities for the meaning of the previously unfamiliar term *electron* are ruled out. A more radical school, instrumentalism, held that, strictly speaking, the theoretical vocabulary remains meaningless. Instrumentalists took scientific theories to be axiomatic systems only part of whose vocabulary—the observational language—is interpreted; the rest is a formal calculus whose purpose is to yield predictions couched in the observational vocabulary. Even instrumentalists, however, were able to maintain a distinction between serious theoretical science and the much-derided meta-physics, for their reconstructions of scientific theories would reveal the uninterpreted vocabulary as playing an important functional role (a result not to be expected in the metaphysical case).

Logical empiricists debated the merits of the two stances, exploring the difficulties of making precise the notion of partial interpretation and the possibility of finding axiomatic systems that would generate all the observational consequences without employing any theoretical vocabulary. Their exchanges were effectively undercut by the American philosopher Hilary Putnam, who recognized that the initial motivation for the approach to theories was deeply problematic. In their brief sketches of the differences between the two languages, logical empiricists had conflated two distinctions. On the one hand there is a contrast between things that can be observed and things that cannot—the observable-unobservable distinction; on the other hand, there is the difference between terms whose meanings can be acquired through demonstration and those whose meanings cannot be acquired in this way—the observational-theoretical distinction. It is a mistake to believe that the distinctions are congruent, that observational terms apply to observable things and theoretical terms to unobservable things. In the first place, many theoretical terms apply to observables (*spectroscope* is an example). More important, many terms learnable through demonstration apply to unobservables—in Putnam's telling example, even small children learn to talk of "people too little to see."

Once the second point was appreciated, the way was open for introducing theoretical vocabulary that logical empiricism had never taken seriously (even though many eminent scientists and gifted science teachers had often

American philosopher Hilary Putnam, who challenged the rationales of logical empiricists by emphasizing the complexity inherent in scientific theory. Courtesy of Hilary Putnam

developed such modes of conveying meaning). One can see that the term *part* might be learned in connection with pieces of observable objects and that its use might cover unobservable things as well, so the specification of atoms as "parts of all matter that themselves have no parts" (whatever its merits today) might have served the contemporaries of John Dalton (1766–1844), an early developer of atomic theory, as a means of appreciating what he was claiming. Logical empiricism lavished great attention on the problem of exposing the structure of scientific theories because solving that problem seemed crucial to the vindication of the theoretical vocabulary employed by the sciences. Putnam showed, in effect, that no such strenuous efforts were required.

THE SEMANTIC CONCEPTION

Starting in the 1960s, philosophers of science explored alternative approaches to scientific theories. Prominent among them was the so-called semantic conception, originally formulated by Patrick Suppes, according to which theories are viewed as collections of models together with hypotheses about how these models relate to parts of nature. Versions of the semantic conception differ in their views about the character of models, sometimes taking models to be abstract mathematical structures, susceptible to precise formal specifications, and sometimes taking them to be more concrete (as chemists do, for example, when they build models of particular molecules).

The semantic conception of theories has several attractive features. First, unlike the older approach, it provides a way of discussing aspects of science that are independent of the choice of a particular language. Second, it appears to do far more justice to areas of science in which theoretical achievements resist axiomatization. Darwinian evolutionary theory is a case in point. During the heyday of the axiomatic approach, a few philosophers attempted to show how the theory of evolution could be brought within the orthodox conception of theories, but their efforts tended to produce formal theories that bordered on triviality. The consequent debates about whether the theory of evolution was more than a tautology should have generated serious philosophical embarrassment. Philosophers deploying the semantic conception, by contrast, shed light on theoretical issues that arise in contemporary evolutionary biology.

Finally, the semantic conception is far better suited to an aspect of the sciences that was frequently neglected, the practice of idealization. Instead of thinking of scientists as aspiring to offer literally correct descriptions of general features of the world, the semantic conception supposes that they propose models accompanied by claims that particular parts of nature correspond to these models in specific respects and to specific degrees.

Digital image depicting Darwin's theory of human evolution.
Mark Bowler/Photo Researchers/Getty Images

THE HISTORICIST CONCEPTION

The work of Thomas S. Kuhn (1922–96) offered a third approach to scientific theories (although some supporters of the semantic conception tried to relate their own proposals to Kuhn's). In his seminal monograph *The Structure of Scientific Revolutions* (1962), Kuhn displaced the term *theory* from its central position in philosophical discussions of the sciences, preferring instead to talk of "paradigms." Although Kuhn's terminology is now omnipresent in popular parlance, he came to regret the locution, partly because of criticism to the effect that his usage of *paradigm* was multiply ambiguous. In his description of everyday scientific work (so-called normal science), however, Kuhn had captured important aspects of theories that philosophers had previously overlooked. He had seen that scientists often draw inspiration from a concrete scientific achievement (the core meaning of *paradigm*) and that this achievement poses research questions for them and often furnishes styles of experimentation or explanation that they aim to emulate. He also saw that scientific work is often dominated by something larger and more enduring than a specific theory: to wit, a program for research that survives through a whole succession of theories. In the wake of Kuhn's work, many philosophers attempted richer descriptions of the scientific background (the "body of theory") on which researchers draw, talking variously of research programs, research traditions, and practices.

What, then, is a scientific theory? In recent decades there have been heated debates about this question. But there is no need to give an answer. In the course of their work, scientists do a wide variety of things. Philosophers of science try to understand aspects of the enterprise,

Thomas Kuhn, the American science historian who questioned the traditional conception of scientific progress by arguing that scientific achievement heavily influences scientific inquiry. Bill Pierce/Time & Life Pictures/Getty Images

offering reconstructions of scientific practice in the hope of addressing particular questions, and there is no reason to think that a particular style of reconstruction will be appropriate to every question. Just as carpenters decide which tools to use on the basis of the job at hand, philosophers might adopt different techniques of reconstruction for different purposes.

When the ways in which meaning accrued to theoretical vocabulary constituted a burning question for the philosophy of science, it was natural to adopt an axiomatic approach to scientific theories and to focus on the connections between theoretical terms and language that are more readily understood (and, to the extent that questions remain in the wake of Putnam's insights about the theoretical-observational and observable-unobservable distinctions, the axiomatic approach can still be of value in this area). Similarly, when a philosopher (or scientist) wonders whether a specific assumption or a particular choice of a parameter value is necessary, the device of axiomatization helps to resolve the question; given an axiomatic presentation, one can explore whether every derivation using the assumption can be transformed into one without. However, when the topic under study is a science in which there are few generalizations, or when one is concerned to elucidate issues about idealization in science, the semantic conception seems much more illuminating. Finally, in probing the dynamics of large-scale change in science—reconstructing the ways in which Darwin won acceptance for his evolutionary theory, for example—the concepts introduced by Kuhn and those who reacted to his work seem more readily applicable. Insistence that there must be a unique answer to what scientific theories really are seems like misplaced dogmatism that obstructs philosophical inquiry.

UNIFICATION AND REDUCTION

One large question about scientific theories that excites philosophical and scientific attention concerns the possibility of producing a single theory that will encompass the domains of all the sciences. Many thinkers are attracted by the idea of a unified science, or by the view that the sciences form a hierarchy. There is a powerful intuitive argument for this attitude. If one considers the subject matter of the social sciences, for example, it seems that social phenomena are the product of people standing in complicated relations to each other and acting in complicated ways. These people, of course, are complex biological and psychological systems. Their psychological activity is grounded in the neural firings in their brains. Hence, people are intricate biological systems. The intricacies of biology are based on the choreography of molecular reactions within and between individual cells. Biology, then, is very complicated chemistry. Chemical reactions themselves involve the forming and breaking of bonds, and these are matters of microphysics. At the end of the day, therefore, all natural phenomena, even those involving interactions between people, are no more than an exceptionally complicated series of transactions between the ultimate physical constituents of matter. A complete account of those ultimate constituents and their interactions would thus amount to a "theory of everything."

This argument builds on some important scientific discoveries. Whereas earlier generations thought that living things must contain something more than complex molecules (some "vital substance," say), or that there must be something more to thinking beings than intricate brains (an "immaterial mind," for example), contemporary biology and contemporary neuroscience showed that there is no need for such hypotheses. Given the firm consensus of contemporary science, there is a constitutive hierarchy: all molecules are made out of fundamental particles; all organic systems are made out of molecules; people are organic systems; and societies are composed of people. Yet there is a difference between a constitutive hierarchy of the things studied by various sciences and a reductive hierarchy of those sciences. Biology studies organisms, entities composed of molecules (and nothing more); it does not follow that biology can be reduced to the science that studies molecules (chemistry).

To understand this distinction it is necessary to have a clear concept of reduction. The most influential such proposal, by Ernest Nagel, was made within the framework of the axiomatic conception of scientific theories. Nagel suggested that one theory is reduced to another when the axioms of the reduced theory can be derived from the axioms of the reducing theory, supplemented with principles ("bridge principles") that connect the language of the reduced theory with that of the reducing theory. So, for example, to reduce genetics to biochemistry, one would show how the principles of genetics follow from premises that include the principles of biochemistry together with specifications in biochemical language of the distinctive vocabulary of genetics (terms such as *gene*, *allele*, and so forth).

Many philosophers criticized the idea of unified science by arguing that, when reduction is understood in Nagel's sense, the constitutive hierarchy does not correspond to a reductive hierarchy. They focused specifically on the possibility of reducing biology to physics and chemistry and of reducing psychology to neuroscience. Attempts at reduction face two major obstacles. First, despite serious efforts to formulate them, there are as yet no bridge principles that link the vocabulary of biology to that of chemistry or the vocabulary of psychology to that of neuroscience. It is evidently hard to think of chemical specifications of the property of being a predator, or neurological specifications of the generic state of desiring to eat ice cream, but the problem arises even in more tractable cases, such as that of providing chemical conditions for being a gene. Every gene is a segment of nucleic acid (DNA in most organisms, RNA in retroviruses); the challenge is to find a chemical condition that distinguishes just those segments of nucleic acid that count as genes. Interestingly, this is a serious research question, for, if it were answered, molecular biologists engaged in genomic sequencing would be able to discover the genes in their sequence data far more rapidly than they are now able to do. The fact that the question is still unanswered is due to the fact that genes are functional units that lack any common chemical structure (beyond being nucleic acids, of course). The language of genetics and the language of chemistry classify the molecules in different ways, and, because of this cross-classification, there is no possibility of reduction.

The second difficulty turns on points about explanation. Imagine a small child who is tired and hot. That child is dragged by a harried parent past an ice-cream stand. The child starts to scream. One might explain this behaviour by saying that the child saw the ice-cream stand and expressed a desire for ice cream, and the parent refused. Suppose further that a friendly neuroscientist is able to trace the causal history of neural firings in the child's brain. Would this replace the everyday explanation? Would it deepen it? Would it even constitute an intelligible account of what had happened? A natural inclination is to suspect that the answer to all these questions is no.

A friend of the unity of science, on the other hand, might respond by claiming that this natural inclination arises only because one is ignorant of the neuroscientific details. If one were able actually to formulate the account of the neural causes and to follow the details of the story, one would obtain greater insight into the child's behaviour and perhaps even be inclined to abandon the explanation based in everyday psychological concepts ("folk psychology").

Once again, the objection to unified science can be posed in a case in which it is possible to give at least some of the biochemical details. One of the best candidates for a regularity in genetics is a revised version of the rule of independent assortment devised by Gregor Mendel (1822–84): genes on different chromosomes are distributed independently when the gametes are formed (at meiosis). Classical (premolecular) genetics provides a satisfying account of why this is so. In sexually reproducing organisms, the gametes (sperm and ova) are formed in a process in which the chromosomes line up in pairs; after some recombination between members of each pair, one chromosome from each pair is transmitted to the gamete. This kind of pairing and separation will produce independent assortments of chromosomal segments (including genes), no matter what the chromosomes are made of and no matter what the underlying molecular mechanisms. If one were now told a complicated story about the sequence of chemical reactions that go on in all instances of meiosis—it would have to be very complicated indeed, since the cases are amazingly diverse—it would add nothing to the original explanation, for it would fail to address the question "Why do genes on different chromosomes assort independently?" The question is completely resolved once one understands that meiosis involves a specific type of pairing and separation.

The points just made do not imply that ventures in molecular biology are unfruitful or that future research in neuroscience will be irrelevant to psychology. To say that not all explanations in genetics can be replaced by molecular accounts is quite compatible with supposing that molecular biology often deepens the perspective offered by classical genetics (as in the cases of mutation, gene replication, gene transcription and translation, and a host of other processes). Moreover, to deny the possibility of reduction in Nagel's sense is not to exclude the possibility that some other notion might allow reducibility on a broader scale. It is important, however, to understand this particular failure of the idea of unified science, because when scientists (and others) often think about a "theory of everything," they are envisaging a set of principles from which explanations of all natural phenomena may be derived. That kind of "final theory" is a pipe dream.

Proponents of the semantic conception of theories explored alternative notions of reduction. For some philosophers, however, conceiving of theories as families of models provided a useful way of capturing what they saw as the piecemeal character of contemporary scientific work. Instead of viewing the sciences as directed at large generalizations, they suggested that researchers offer a patchwork of models, successful in different respects and to different degrees at characterizing the behaviour of bits and pieces of the natural world. This theme was thoroughly pursued by the American philosopher Nancy Cartwright, who emerged in the late 20th century as the most vigorous critic of unified science.

Cartwright opposed "vertical reduction," but she believed that the standard critiques did not go far enough. She argued that philosophers should also be skeptical of "horizontal reduction," the idea that models and generalizations have broad scope. Traditional philosophy of science took for granted the possibility of extrapolating regularities beyond the limited contexts in which they can be successfully applied. As a powerful illustration, Cartwright invited readers to consider their confidence in Newton's second law, which states that force is equal to the product of mass and acceleration. The law can be used to account for the motions of particular kinds of bodies; more exactly, the solar system, the pendulum, and so forth can be modeled as Newtonian systems. There are many natural settings, however, in which it is hard to create Newtonian order. Imagine, for example, someone dropping a piece of paper money from a high window overlooking a public square. Does Newton's second law determine the trajectory? A standard response would be that it does in principle, though in practice the forces operating would be exceedingly hard to specify. Cartwright questioned whether this reponse is correct. She suggested instead that modern science should be thought of in terms of a history of successful building of Newtonian models for a limited range of situations and that it is only a "fundamentalist faith" that such models can be applied everywhere and always. It is consistent with current scientific knowledge, she argued, that the world is thoroughly "dappled," containing some pockets of order in which modeling works well and pockets of disorder that cannot be captured by the kinds of models that human beings can formulate.

CHAPTER 3

CHANGE AND THE EFFECT ON SCIENTIFIC REALISM

A lthough some proposals were influenced by the critical reaction to logical empiricism, the topics are those that figured on the logical-empiricist agenda. In many philosophical circles, that agenda continues to be central to the philosophy of science, sometimes accompanied by the dismissal of critiques of logical empiricism and sometimes by an attempt to integrate critical insights into the discussion of traditional questions. For some philosophers, however, the philosophy of science was profoundly transformed by a succession of criticisms that began in the 1950s as some historically minded scholars pondered issues about scientific change.

The historicist critique was initiated by the philosophers N.R. Hanson (1924–67), Stephen Toulmin, Paul Feyerabend (1924–94), and Thomas Kuhn. Although these authors differed on many points, they shared the view that standard logical-empiricist accounts of confirmation, theory, and other topics were quite inadequate to explain the major transitions that have occurred in the history of the sciences. Feyerabend, the most radical and flamboyant of the group, put the fundamental challenge with characteristic brio: if one seeks a methodological rule that will account for all of the historical episodes that philosophers of science are inclined to celebrate—the triumph of the Copernican system, the birth of modern chemistry, the Darwinian revolution, the transition to the theories of relativity, and so forth—then the best candidate is "anything goes." Even in less-provocative forms, however, philosophical reconstructions of parts of the history of science had the effect of calling into question the very concepts of scientific progress and rationality.

A natural conception of scientific progress is that it consists in the accumulation of truth. In the heyday of logical empiricism, a more qualified version might have seemed preferable: scientific progress consists in accumulating truths in the "observation language." Philosophers of science in this period also thought that they had a clear view of scientific rationality: to be rational is to accept and reject hypotheses according to the rules of method, or perhaps to distribute degrees of confirmation in accordance with Bayesian standards. The historicist challenge consisted in arguing, with respect to detailed historical examples, that the very transitions in which great scientific advances seem to be made cannot be seen as the result of the simple accumulation of truth. Further, the participants in the major scientific controversies of the past did not divide neatly into irrational losers and rational winners; all too frequently, it was suggested, the heroes flouted the canons of rationality, while the reasoning of the supposed reactionaries was exemplary.

THE WORK OF THOMAS KUHN

In the 1960s it was unclear which version of the historicist critique would have the most impact, but during subsequent decades Kuhn's monograph emerged as the seminal text. *The Structure of Scientific Revolutions* offered a general pattern of scientific change. Inquiries in a given field start with a clash of different perspectives. Eventually one approach manages to resolve some concrete issue, and investigators concur in pursuing it—they follow the "paradigm." Commitment to the approach begins a tradition of normal science in which there are well-defined problems, or "puzzles," for researchers to solve. In the practice of normal science, the failure to solve a puzzle does not reflect badly on the paradigm but rather does so on the skill of the researcher. Only when puzzles repeatedly prove recalcitrant does the community begin to develop a sense that something may be amiss; the unsolved puzzles acquire a new status, being seen as anomalies. Even so, the normal scientific tradition will continue so long as there are no available alternatives. If a rival does emerge, and if it succeeds in attracting a new consensus, then a revolution occurs: the old paradigm is replaced by a new one, and investigators pursue a new normal scientific tradition. Puzzle solving is now directed by the victorious paradigm, and the old pattern may be repeated, with some puzzles deepening into anomalies and generating a sense of crisis, which ultimately gives way to a new revolution, a new normal scientific tradition, and so on indefinitely.

Kuhn's proposals can be read in a number of ways. Many scientists have found that his account of normal science offers insights into their own experiences and that the idea of puzzle solving is particularly apt. In addition, from a strictly historical perspective, Kuhn offered a novel historiography of the sciences. However, although a few scholars attempted to apply his approach, most historians of science were skeptical of Kuhnian categories. Philosophers of science, on the other hand, focused neither on his suggestions about normal science nor on his general historiography, concentrating instead on Kuhn's

The cover of Thomas Kuhn's The Structure of Scientific Revolutions. *The book is considered one of the 20th century's most influential works of history and philosophy.* **The University of Chicago Press**

treatment of the episodes he termed "revolutions." For it is in discussing scientific revolutions that he challenged traditional ideas about progress and rationality.

At the basis of the challenge is Kuhn's claim that paradigms are incommensurable with each other. His complicated notion of incommensurability begins from a mathematical metaphor, alluding to the Pythagorean discovery of numbers (such as $\sqrt{2}$) that could not be expressed as rationals; irrational and rational lengths share no common measure. He considered three aspects of the incommensurability of paradigms (which he did not always clearly separate). First, paradigms are conceptually incommensurable in that the languages in which they describe nature cannot readily be translated into one another; communication in revolutionary debates, he suggested, is inevitably partial. Second, paradigms are observationally incommensurable in that workers in different paradigms will respond in different ways to the same stimuli—or, as he sometimes put it, they will see different things when looking in the same places. Third, paradigms are methodologically incommensurable in that they have different criteria for success, attributing different values to questions and to proposed ways of answering them. In combination, Kuhn argued, these forms of incommensurability are so deep that, after a scientific revolution, there will be a sense in which scientists work in a different world.

These striking claims are defended by considering a small number of historical examples of revolutionary change. Kuhn focused most on the Copernican revolution, on the replacement of the phlogiston theory with Lavoisier's new chemistry, and on the transition from Newton's physics to the special and general theories of relativity. So, for example, he supported the doctrine of conceptual incommensurability by arguing that pre-Copernican astronomy could make no sense of the Copernican notion of planet (within the earlier astronomy, the Earth itself could not be a planet), that phlogiston chemistry could make no sense of Lavoisier's notion of oxygen (for phlogistonians, combustion is a process in which phlogiston is emitted, and talk of oxygen as a substance that is absorbed is quite wrongheaded), and that theories of relativity distinguish two notions of mass (rest mass and proper mass), neither of which makes sense in Newtonian terms.

All of these arguments received detailed philosophical attention, and it became apparent that the conclusions can be met by adopting a more sophisticated approach to language than that presupposed by Kuhn. The crucial issue is whether the languages of rival paradigms suffice to identify the objects and properties referred to in the terms of the other. Although Kuhn was right to see difficulties here, it is an exaggeration to suppose that the identification is impossible. From Lavoisier's perspective, for example, the antiquated term *dephlogisticated air* sometimes means "what remains when phlogiston is removed from the air" (in which case, because there is no such substance as phlogiston, the term fails to pick out anything in the world). But at other times it is used to designate a specific gas (oxygen) that both groups of chemists have isolated. As far as conceptual incommensurability is concerned, it is possible to see Kuhn's examples as cases in which communication is tricky but not impossible and in which the parties respond to and talk about a common world.

The thesis of observational incommensurability is best illustrated via Kuhn's example of the Copernican revolution. In the late 16th century, Johannes Kepler (1571–1630), a committed follower of Copernicus, assisted the great astronomer Tycho Brahe (1546–1601), who believed that the Earth is at rest. Kuhn imagined Tycho and Kepler watching the sunrise together, and, like Hanson before him, suggested that Tycho would see a moving Sun coming into view, while Kepler would see a static Sun becoming visible as the Earth rotates.

Evidently Tycho and Kepler might report their visual experiences in different ways. Nor should it be supposed that there is some privileged "primitive" language—a language that picks out shapes and colours, perhaps—in which all observers can describe what they see and reach agreement with those who are similarly situated. But these points, while they may have been neglected in earlier philosophy of science, do not yield the radical Kuhnian conclusions. In the first place, the difference in the experiential reports is quite compatible with the perception of a common object, possibly described correctly by one of

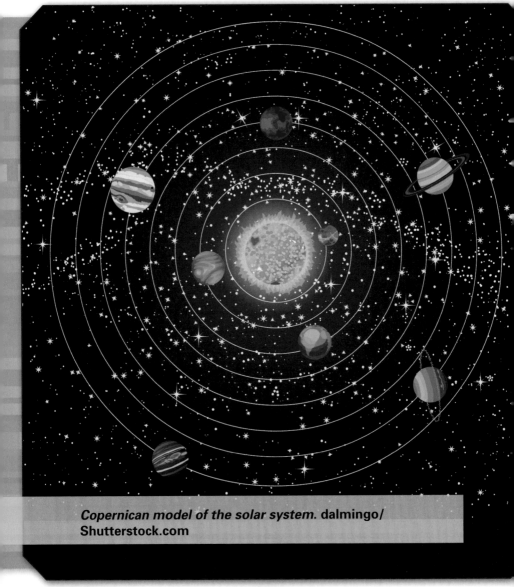

Copernican model of the solar system. dalmingo/ Shutterstock.com

the participants, possibly accurately reported by neither; both Tycho and Kepler see the Sun, and both perceive the relative motion of Sun and Earth. Furthermore, although there may be no bedrock language of uncontaminated observation to which they can retreat, they have available to them forms of description that presuppose only shared commonsense ideas about objects in the vicinity. If they become tired of exchanging their preferred reports— "I see a moving Sun," "I see a stationary Sun becoming visible through the Earth's rotation"—they can both agree that the orange blob above the hillside is the Sun and that more of it can be seen now than could be seen two minutes ago. There is no reason, then, to deny that Tycho and Kepler experience the same world or to suppose that there are no observable aspects of it about which they can reach agreement.

The thesis of methodological incommensurability can also be illustrated through the Copernican example. After the publication of Copernicus's system in 1543, professional astronomers quickly realized that, for any Sun-centred system like Copernicus's, it would be possible to produce an equally accurate Earth-centred system, and conversely. How could the debate be resolved? One difference between the systems lay in the number of technical devices required to generate accurate predictions of planetary motions. Copernicus did better on this score, using fewer of the approved repertoire of geometrical tricks than his opponents did. But there was also a tradition of arguments against the possibility of a moving Earth. Scholars had long maintained, for example, that, if the Earth moved, objects released from high places would fall backwards, birds and clouds would be left behind, loose materials on the Earth's surface would be flung off, and so forth. Given the then-current state of theories of motion, there were no obvious errors in these lines of reasoning. Hence, it might have seemed that a decision about the Earth's motion must involve a judgment of values (perhaps to the effect that it is more important not to introduce dynamical absurdities than to reduce the number of technical astronomical devices). Or perhaps the decision could be made only on faith—faith that answers to questions about the behaviour of birds and clouds would eventually be found.

Methodological incommensurability presents the most severe challenge to views about progress and rationality in the sciences. In effect, Kuhn offered a different version of the underdetermination thesis, one more firmly grounded in the actual practice of the sciences. Instead of supposing that any theory has rivals that make exactly the same predictions and accord equally well with all canons of scientific method, Kuhn suggested that certain kinds of large controversies in the history of science pit against each other approaches with different virtues and defects and that there is no privileged way to balance virtues and defects. The only way to address this challenge is to probe the examples, trying to understand the ways in which various kinds of trade-offs might be defended or criticized.

RESPONSES

One way to think about the Copernican example (and other Kuhnian revolutions) is to recognize the evolution of the debates. In 1543 the controversy might have seemed quite unsettled; the simplification of technical machinery might have inspired some people to work further on the Copernican program, while the dynamical problems posed by the moving Earth might have prompted others to articulate the more traditional view. If neither choice can be seen as uniquely rational, neither can be dismissed as unreasonable.

Later, after Kepler's proposals of elliptical orbits, Galileo's telescopic observations, and Galileo's consideration of the dynamical arguments, the balance shifted. Copernicanism had shed a number of its defects, while the traditional view had acquired some new ones. Since both approaches still faced residual problems—sciences rarely solve all the problems that lie within their domain, and there are always unanswered questions—it would still have been possible in principle to give greater weight to the virtues of traditional astronomy or to the defects of Copernicanism. By the mid-17th century, however, it would have been unreasonable to adopt any value judgment that saw the achievements of the tradition as so glorious, or the deficiencies of the rival as so severe, that Copernicanism should still be rejected. That type of valuation would be akin to preferring a decrepit jalopy, with a nonfunctioning engine and a rusting chassis, to a serviceable new car solely on the grounds that the old wreck had a more appealing hood ornament.

Although a few philosophers of science tried to make this line of response to Kuhn's challenge more general and more precise, many contemporary discussions seem to embody one of two premature reactions. Some hold that the worries about revolutionary change have been adequately addressed and that the philosophy of science can return to business as usual. Others conclude that Kuhn's arguments are definitive and that there is no hope of salvaging the progressiveness and rationality of science.

Kuhn's discussions of incommensurability challenge claims about the rationality of science by asking whether it is possible to show how the accepted views of method and justification would allow the resolution of scientific revolutions. The philosophical task here is to adapt one of the existing approaches to confirmation (Bayesianism or eliminativism, for example) to the complex contexts Kuhn presents or, if that cannot be done, to formulate new methodological rules, rules that can be defended as conditions of rationality that will apply to these contexts.

Equally, the points about incommensurability challenge the thesis that the sciences are progressive by denying the possibility of understanding the history of science as a process of accumulating truth. Here the philosopher of science needs to provide an account of progress in terms of convergence on the truth or to show how progress can be understood in other terms.

In the wake of Kuhn's work, all of these options have been pursued. Beginning from within a Popperian framework, the Hungarian-born philosopher Imre Lakatos (1922–74) attempted to provide a "methodology of research programmes" that would understand progress in terms of increasing the "truth content" of scientific theories. The American philosopher Larry Laudan tried to show how it is possible to think of scientific progress in terms of "problem solving," and he offered a methodology of science based on the assessment of problem-solving success. Unfortunately, however, it seems difficult to make sense of the notion of a solution to a problem without some invocation of the concept of truth; the most obvious account of what it is to solve a scientific problem identifies a solution with a true answer to a question.

SCIENTIFIC REALISM

The dominant position among those philosophers who tried to explain the notion of scientific progress, not

surprisingly, was to try to rehabilitate ideas of convergence to the truth in the face of worries that neither truth
nor convergence can be made sense of. This fueled a wide-
ranging dispute over the viability of scientific realism, one
that engaged philosophers, historians, and other students
of science.

Issues about scientific realism had already emerged
within the logical-empiricist discussions of scientific theories. Philosophers who held that theoretical language was
strictly meaningless, taking theories to be instruments for
the prediction of statements formulated in an observational vocabulary, concluded that the theoretical claims of
the sciences lack truth value (i.e., are neither true nor false)
and that use of the formalism of theoretical science does
not commit one to the existence of unobservable entities. Instrumentalists suggested that terms such as *electron*
should not be taken to refer to minute parts of matter;
they simply function in a formal calculus that enables one
to make true predictions about observables. By contrast,
philosophers who emphasized the explanatory power
of scientific theories argued that one cannot make sense of
theoretical explanation unless one recognizes the reality
of unobservable entities; one can understand the character of chemical bonds and see why elements combine
in the ways they do if one takes the proposals about elec-
trons filling shells around nuclei seriously but not if one
supposes that *electron*, *shell*, and *nucleus* are mere façons
de parler.

An initial dispute about scientific realism thus
focused on the status of unobservables. In an obvious
sense this was a debate about democracy with respect
to scientific language: realists and instrumentalists alike
believed that the concept of truth made good sense
for a portion of scientific language—the observation

REALISM VS. INSTRUMENTALISM

The dispute between scientific realists and antirealists, though often associated with conflicting ontological attitudes toward the unobserved (and perhaps unobservable) entities ostensibly postulated by some scientific theories, primarily concerns the status of the theories themselves and what scientists should be seen as trying to accomplish in propounding them. Both sides are agreed that, to be acceptable, a scientific theory should "save the phenomena"—that is, it should at least be consistent with, and ideally facilitate correct prediction of, such matters of observable fact as may be recorded in reports of relevant observations and, where appropriate, experiments. The issue concerns whether theories can and should be seen as attempting more than this. Realists, notably including Karl Popper, J.J.C. Smart, Ian Hacking, and Hilary Putnam, along with many others, have claimed that they should be so viewed: Science aims, in its theories, at a literally true account of what the world is like, and accepting those theories involves accepting their ingredient theoretical claims as true descriptions of aspects of reality—perhaps themselves not open to observation—additional to and underlying the phenomena.

Against this, the doctrine of instrumentalism claims that scientific theories are no more than devices, or "instruments" (in effect, sets of inference rules) for generating predictions about observable phenomena from evidence about such phenomena. This claim can be understood in two ways. It could be that theoretical scientific statements are not, despite appearances, genuine statements at all but rules of inference in disguise, so that the question of their truth (or falsehood) simply does not arise. In this case, instrumentalism is akin to expressivism about ethical statements. Alternatively, it could be that, as far as the aims of science go, what matters when evaluating a scientific theory—given that it meets other desiderata such as simplicity, economy, generality of application, and so on—is only its inferential (or instrumental) reliability; its truth or falsehood is of no scientific concern. A notable development of the latter approach is the constructive empiricism of Bas van Fraassen, according to which science aims not at true theories but at theories which are "empirically adequate," in the sense that they capture or predict relevant truths about observable matters.

Antirealism about science, both in its earlier instrumentalist form and in van Fraassen's version, clearly relies upon a fundamental distinction between statements which are, and those which are not, wholly about observable entities or states of affairs. Realists frequently deny the tenability of this distinction, arguing that there is no "theory-neutral" language in which observations may be reported, or at any rate that there is no sharp, principled division between what is observable and what is not.

language—though they differed as to whether this privileged status should be extended to scientific language as a whole.

EARLY ARGUMENTS FOR REALISM

During the 1960s and '70s, a number of developments tipped the controversy in favour of the realists. First was Putnam's diagnosis that the logical-empiricist account of the meanings of theoretical terms rested on conflating two distinctions. Second was the increasing acceptance, in the wake of the writings of Kuhn and Hanson, of the view that there is no neutral observation language. If all language bears theoretical presuppositions, then there seems to be no basis for supposing that language purporting to talk about unobservables must be treated differently from language about observables. Third was an influential argument by the American philosopher Grover Maxwell (1918–81), who noted that the concept of the observable varies with the range of available devices: many people are unable to observe much without interposing pieces of glass (or plastic) between their eyes and the world; more can be observed if one uses magnifying glasses, microscopes, telescopes, and other devices. Noting that there is an apparent continuum here, Maxwell asked where one should mark the decisive ontological shift: at what point should one not count as real the entities one thinks one is observing?

Perhaps most decisive was a line of reasoning that became known as "the ultimate argument for realism," which appeared in two major versions. One version, developed by Salmon, considered in some detail the historical process through which scientists had convinced themselves of the reality of atoms. Focusing on the work of the French physicist Jean Perrin (1870–1942), Salmon noted that there were many, apparently independent, methods of determining the values of quantities pertaining to alleged unobservables, each of which supplied the same answer, and he argued that this would be an extraordinary coincidence if the unobservables did not in fact exist. The second version, elaborated by J.J.C. Smart, Putnam, and Richard Boyd, was even more influential. Here, instead of focusing on independent ways of determining a theoretical quantity, realists pointed to the existence of theories that give rise to systematic successes over a broad domain, such as the computation of the energies of reactions with extraordinary accuracy or the manufacture of organisms with precise and highly unusual traits. Unless these theories were at least approximately true, realists argued, the successes they give rise to would amount to a coincidence of cosmic proportions—a sheer miracle.

THE ANTIREALISM OF VAN FRAASSEN, LAUDAN, AND FINE

In the 1990s, however, the controversy about the reality of unobservables was revived through the development of sophisticated antirealist arguments. Van Fraassen advocated a position that he called "constructive empiricism," a view intended to capture the insights of logical empiricism while avoiding its defects. A champion of the semantic conception of theories, he proposed that scientists build models that are designed to "save the phenomena" by yielding correct predictions about observables. To adopt the models is simply to suppose that observable events and states of affairs are as if the models were true, but there is no need to commit oneself to the existence of the unobservable entities and processes that figure in the models. Rather, one should remain agnostic. Because the aim of science is to achieve correct predictions about observables, there is no need to assume the extra risks involved in commitment to the existence of unobservables.

A different antirealist argument, presented by Laudan, attacks directly the "ultimate argument" for realism. Laudan reflected on the history of science and considered all the past theories that were once counted as outstandingly successful. He offered a list of outmoded theories, claiming that all enjoyed successes and noting that not only is each now viewed as false, but each also contains theoretical vocabulary that is now recognized as picking out nothing at all in nature. If so many scientists of past generations judged their theories to be successful and, on that basis, concluded that they were true, and if, by current lights, they were all wrong, how can it be supposed that the contemporary situation is different—that, when contemporary scientists gesture at apparent successes and infer to the approximate truth of their theories, they are correct? Laudan formulated a "pessimistic induction on the history of science," generalizing from the fact that large numbers of past successful theories have proved false to the conclusion that successful contemporary theories are also incorrect.

A third antirealist objection, formulated by both Laudan and Arthur Fine, charges that the popular defenses of realism beg the question. Realists try to convince their opponents by suggesting that only a realist view of unobservables will explain the success of science. In doing so, however, they presuppose that the fact that a certain doctrine has explanatory power provides a reason to accept it. But the point of many antirealist arguments is that allegations about explanatory power have no bearing on questions of truth. Antirealists are unpersuaded when it is suggested, for example, that a hypothesis about atoms should be accepted because it explains observable chemical phenomena. They will be equally unmoved when they are told that a philosophical hypothesis (the hypothesis of scientific realism) should be accepted because it explains the success of science. In both instances, they want to know why the features of the hypotheses to which realists draw attention—the ability of those hypotheses to generate correct conclusions about observable matters—should be taken as indicators of the truth of the hypotheses.

"PIECEMEAL" REALISM

Realists tried to respond to these powerful points. One popular rejoinder is that antirealists cannot account for important facets of scientific practice. Thus, it is sometimes suggested that the routine method of conjoining theoretical claims from different scientific theories (as, for example, when earth scientists draw on parts of physics and chemistry) would not make sense unless there was a serious commitment to the approximate truth of the theoretical principles. Alternatively, one may take the practice of choosing certain kinds of experiments (experiments taken to be particularly revealing) to reflect a belief in the reality of underlying entities; thus, a medical researcher might choose a particular class of animals to inject with an antibiotic on the grounds that the concentration of bacteria in those animals is likely to be especially high.

Or the realist can attempt to argue that the kinds of inferences that the antirealist will acknowledge as unproblematic—for example, the generalization from observed samples to conclusions about a broader population of observable things—can be made only in light of an understanding of unobservable entities and mechanisms. One cannot tell what makes a sample suitable for generalization unless one has views about the ways in which that sample might be biased, and that will typically entail beliefs about relevant unobservable causes. Antirealists must either show that they have the resources to make sense of these and other features of scientific practice or offer reasons for thinking that the procedures in question should be revised.

Laudan's pessimistic induction on the history of science attracted considerable scrutiny. Realists pointed out, correctly, that his list of successful past theories contains a number of dubious entries. Thus, it would be hard to defend the medieval theory of disease as caused by an imbalance of humours as particularly successful, and similar judgments apply to the geological catastrophism of the 18th century and the phlogiston theory of chemical combination.

Yet it is impossible to dismiss all of Laudan's examples. One of his most telling points is that the account of the wave propagation of light of Augustin-Jean Fresnel (1788–1827) was spectacularly successful in explaining and predicting facts about diffraction and interference; one of its most dramatic successes, for example, was the prediction of the Poisson bright spot, a point of light at the centre of the shadow of a small rotating disk. (Ironically, the French mathematician for whom

Augustin-Jean Fresnel, detail of an engraving by Ambroise Tardieu after a contemporary portrait, 1825. H. Roger-Viollet

the spot is named, Siméon-Denis Poisson [1781–1840], believed that Fresnel was wrong and that the prediction of the spot was an absurd consequence of a false theory.) Fresnel, however, based his theory on the hypothesis that light waves are propagated in an all-pervading ether. Since contemporary science rejects the ether, it must also reject Fresnel's theory as false.

This example is especially instructive because it points to a refinement of realism. Contemporary optics takes over Fresnel's mathematical treatment of wave propagation but denies the need for any medium in which the propagation takes place. So part of his theory is honoured as approximately correct, while the rest is seen as going astray because of Fresnel's belief that any wave motion needs a medium in which the waves are propagated. Faced with a choice between saying that Fresnel's theory is correct and saying that it is wrong, contemporary scientists would opt for the negative verdict. One would do greater justice to the situation, however, not by treating the theory as a whole but by judging some parts to be true and others false. Furthermore, when Fresnel's work is analyzed in this way, it can be seen that the correct parts are responsible for its predictive successes. Appeals to the ether play no role when Fresnel is accounting for experimental data about interference bands and diffraction patterns. Hence, this example supports the realist linkage of success and truth by revealing that the parts of theory actually put to work in generating successful predictions continue to be counted as correct.

Indeed, realists can go farther than this: it can be argued that there is empirical evidence, of a kind that antirealists should be prepared to accept, of a connection between success and truth. People sometimes find themselves in situations in which their success at a particular task depends on their views about observable entities that they are temporarily unable to observe (think, for example, about card games in which players have to make judgments about cards that other players are holding). The evidence from such situations shows that systematic success is dependent on forming approximately correct hypotheses about the hidden things. There are no good grounds for thinking that the regularity breaks down when the entities in question lie below the threshold of human observation. Indeed, it would be a strange form of metaphysical hubris to suppose that the world is set up so that the connection between success and truth is finely tuned to the contingent perceptual powers of human beings.

The debate about the reality of the unobservable entities that scientific theories frequently posit is not over, but realism is once again a dominant position. The contemporary realist view, however, was refined by the critiques of van Fraassen, Laudan, and Fine. The most plausible version of realism is a "piecemeal realism," a view that defends the permissibility of interpreting talk of unobservables literally but insists on attention to the details of particular cases. Realists also learned to give up the thought that theories as wholes should be assessed as true or false. They thus contend for the acceptance of particular unobservable entities and for the approximate truth of particular claims about those entities.

SCIENTIFIC TRUTH

"Piecemeal realism" represents only one of the controversies that surround scientific realism, namely the debate about whether talk of unobservables should have the same status as talk of observables. Contemporary exchanges, however, are often directed at a broader issue: the possibility of judging whether any claim at all is true. Some of these exchanges involve issues that are as old as philosophy—very general questions about the nature and possibility of truth. Others arise from critiques of traditional philosophy of science that are often inspired by the work of Kuhn but are more radical.

Many people, including many philosophers, find it natural to think of truth as correspondence to reality. The picture they endorse takes human language (and thought) to pick out things and properties in a mind-independent world and supposes that what people say (or think) is true just in case the things they pick out have the properties they attribute to them. A deep and ancient conundrum is how words (or thoughts) manage to be connected with determinate parts of nature. It is plainly impossible for human beings ever to occupy a position from which they could observe simultaneously both their language (thought) and the mind-independent world and establish (or ascertain) the connection. That impossibility led many thinkers (including Kuhn, in a rare but influential discussion of truth) to wonder whether the idea of truth as correspondence to mind-independent reality makes sense.

The issues here are complex and reach into technical areas of metaphysics and the philosophy of language. Some philosophers maintain that a correspondence theory of truth can be developed and defended without presupposing any absurd Archimedean point from which correspondences are instituted or detected. Others believe that it is a mistake to pursue any theory of truth at all. To assert that a given statement is true, they argue, is merely another way of asserting the statement itself. Fine elaborated this idea further in the context of the philosophy of science, proposing that one should accept neither realism nor antirealism; rather, one should give up talking about truth in connection with scientific hypotheses and adopt what he calls the "natural ontological attitude." To adopt that attitude is simply to endorse the claims made by contemporary science without indulging in the unnecessary philosophical flourish of declaring them to be "true."

These sophisticated proposals and the intricate arguments urged in favour of them contrast with a more widely accessible critique of the idea of "scientific truth" that also starts from Kuhn's suspicion that the idea of truth as correspondence to mind-independent reality makes no sense. Inspired by Kuhn's recognition of the social character of scientific knowledge (a paradigm is, after all, something that is shared by a community), a number of scholars proposed a more thoroughly sociological approach to science. Urging that beliefs acclaimed as "true" or "false" be explained in the same ways, they concluded that truth must be relativized to communities: a statement counts as true for a community just in case members of that community accept it.

The proposal for a serious sociology of scientific knowledge should be welcomed. As the sociologists David Bloor and Barry Barnes argued in the early 1970s, it is unsatisfactory to suppose that only beliefs counted as incorrect need social and psychological explanation. For it would be foolish to suggest that human minds have some attraction to the truth and that cases in which people go astray must be accounted for in terms of the operation of social or psychological biases that interfere with this natural aptitude. All human beliefs have psychological causes, and those causes typically involve facts about the societies in which the people in question live. A comprehensive account of how an individual scientist came to some novel conclusion would refer not only to the observations and inferences that he made but to the ways in which he was trained, the range of options available for pursuing inquiries, and the values that guided various choices—all of which would lead, relatively quickly, to aspects of the social practice of the surrounding community. Barnes and Bloor were right to advocate symmetry, to see all beliefs as subject to psychological and sociological explanation.

But nothing momentous follows from this. Consistent with the emphasis on symmetry, as so far understood, one could continue to draw the everyday distinction between those forms of observation, inference, and social coordination that tend to generate correct beliefs and those that typically lead to error. The clear-eyed observer and the staggering drunkard may both come to believe that there is an elephant in the room, and psychological accounts may be offered of the belief-formation process in each case. This does not mean, of course, that one is compelled to treat the two belief-forming processes as on a par, viewing them as equally reliable in detecting aspects of reality. So one can undertake the enterprise of seeking the psychological and social causes of scientific belief without abandoning the distinction between those that are well-grounded and those that are not.

Sociological critiques of "scientific truth" sometimes try to reach their radical conclusions by offering a crude analogue of Laudan's historical argument against scientific realism. They point out that different contemporary societies hold views that are at variance with Western scientific doctrines; indigenous Polynesian people may have ideas about inheritance, for example, that are at odds with those enshrined in genetics. To insist that Westerners are right and the Polynesians wrong, it is suggested, is to overlook the fact of "natural rationality," to suppose that there is a difference in psychological constitution that favours Westerners.

But this reasoning is fallacious. Sometimes differences in people's beliefs can be explained by citing differences in their sensory faculties or intellectual acumen. Such cases, however, are relatively rare. The typical account of why disagreement occurs identifies differences in experiences or interests. Surely this is the right way to approach the divergence of Westerners and Polynesians on issues of heredity. To hold that Western views on this particular topic are more likely to be right than Polynesian views is not to suppose that Westerners are individually brighter (in fact, a compelling case can be made for thinking that, on average, people who live in less-pampered conditions are more intelligent) but rather to point out that Western science has taken a sustained collective interest in questions of heredity and that it has organized considerable resources to acquire experiences that Polynesians do not share. So, when one invokes the "ultimate argument for realism" and uses the success of contemporary molecular genetics to infer the approximate truth of the underlying ideas about heredity, one is not arrogantly denying the natural rationality of the Polynesians. On the contrary, Westerners should be willing to defer to them on topics that they have investigated and Westerners have not.

Yet another attempt to argue that the only serviceable notion of truth reduces to social consensus begins from the strong Quinean thesis of the underdetermination of theories by experience. Some historians and sociologists of science maintained that choices of doctrine and method are always open in the course of scientific practice. Those choices are made not by appealing to evidence but by drawing on antecedently accepted social values or, in some instances, by simultaneously "constructing" both the natural and the social order. The best versions of these arguments attempt to specify in some detail what the relevant alternatives are; in such cases, as with Kuhn's arguments about the irresolvability of scientific revolutions, philosophical responses must attend to the details.

Unfortunately, such detailed specifications are relatively rare, and the usual strategy is for the sociological critique to proceed by invoking the general thesis of underdetermination and to declare that there are always rival ways of going on. As noted earlier, however, a blanket claim about inevitable underdetermination is highly suspect, and without it sociological confidence in "truth by consensus" is quite unwarranted.

Issues about scientific realism and the proper understanding of truth remain unsettled. It is important, however, to appreciate what the genuine philosophical options are. Despite its popularity in the history and sociology of science, the crude sociological reduction of truth is not among those options. Yet, like history, the sociological study of science can offer valuable insights for philosophers to ponder.

SCIENCE, SOCIETY, AND VALUES

Scientific inquiry does not exist in a vacuum. From the work of the Vienna Circle to any laboratory at any university today, science is something done as a collective endeavour. Underlying principles and basic social beliefs—whether held by an individual or a group— unavoidably colour scientific processes and conclusions and therefore deserve to be given weight in any discussion of the philosophy of science.

SCIENCE AS A SOCIAL ACTIVITY

Traditional philosophy of science is relentlessly individualistic. It focuses on individual agents and on the conditions they should satisfy if their beliefs are to be properly supported. On the face of it, this is a curious limitation, for it is evident that contemporary science (and most science of the past) is a social activity. Scientists rely on each other for results, samples, techniques, and many other things. Their interactions are often cooperative, sometimes competitive. Moreover, in the societies in which most scientific research is carried out, the coordinated work of science is embedded in a web of social relations that links laboratories to government agencies, to educational institutions, and to groups of citizens. Can philosophy of science simply ignore this social setting?

Many philosophers believe that it can. It is worth recalling, however, that one of the principal influences on the development of modern science, Francis Bacon, was explicitly concerned with science as a social endeavour and that the founders of the Royal Society attempted to create an institution that would follow Bacon's direction. Furthermore, the notion of social (or collective) rationality is philosophically important. As of 1543, the choice between Copernicanism and the traditional Earth-centred astronomy was unclear; the discussion evolved because some scientists were willing to commit themselves to exploring each of the two views. That was a good thing— but the good was a feature of the community and not of the individuals. Had one of the rival positions languished and all of the community members dedicated themselves to a single point of view, it would have been hard to accuse any single individual of a failure of rationality. It would not, however, have been a rational community.

The social dimension of science calls for a broader approach to rationality than what is standard in philosophical discussions. One way of understanding why some methods or principles deserve the label "rational" is to suggest that the ultimate standard for appraising them is in terms of their capacity to yield true beliefs. By the same token, one could suppose that institutions or methods of organizing inquiry count as rational if they are likely to enhance the chances of a future state in which members of the community believe the truth.

It is not hard to think of ways of promoting diversity (broadly defined) in a scientific community. Perhaps the

THE ROYAL SOCIETY OF LONDON

The oldest national scientific society in the world and the leading national organization for the promotion of scientific research in Britain, the Royal Society of London originated on November 28, 1660. Twelve men met after a lecture at Gresham College, London, by Christopher Wren (then professor of astronomy at the college) and resolved to set up "a Colledge for the promoting of Physico-Mathematicall Experimentall Learning." Those present included the scientists Robert Boyle and Bishop John Wilkins, as well as the courtiers Sir Robert Moray and William, 2nd Viscount Brouncker. Brouncker went on to become the Royal Society's first president.

The initiative had various more or less close precursors, including a group that met in London in 1645, the Oxford "Experimental Philosophy Club" in the 1650s, and correspondence networks such as that of the reformer and philanthropist Samuel Hartlib. Yet the body set up in 1660 was consciously new, with ambitions to become a truly national society devoted

Carlton House Terrace in Westminster, London, home of the Royal Society since 1967. © iStockphoto/Thinkstock

to the promotion of science. These ambitions were put into effect over the next few years, particularly through a charter of incorporation granted by Charles II in 1662 and revised in 1663. The royal charter provided an institutional structure for the society, with president, treasurer, secretaries, and council. Though it had royal patronage almost from the start, the society has always remained a voluntary organization, independent of the British state.

From the outset the society aspired to combine the role of research institute with that of clearinghouse for knowledge and forum for arbitration, though the latter function became dominant after the society's earliest years. A key development was the establishment in 1665 of a periodical that acted as the society's mouthpiece (though it was actually published by the secretary, initially Henry Oldenburg, and was only officially adopted by the society in 1753): this was the *Philosophical Transactions*, which still flourishes today as the oldest scientific journal in continuous publication.

educational system could encourage some people to take large risks and others to pursue relatively safe strategies. Perhaps the system of rewards for scientific achievement could be set up in such a way that individuals would gravitate to lines of research that looked neglected. Standard techniques of mathematical modeling reveal that institutional structures like these produce collectively rational outcomes in situations that seem to recur in the history of the sciences. One thus discovers that factors one might have thought of as antithetical to the rational pursuit of truth—individual biases or interest in social rewards—actually play a positive role in the collective venture.

Detailed sociological investigation is required to discover the ways in which scientists interact with each other and with parts of the broader society; detailed psychological investigations are needed to understand the ways in which they make choices. A satisfactory philosophical account of the sciences should be just as interested in whether the sociopsychological matrix is conducive to the attainment of truth by the community as it is in whether particular lines or styles of reasoning lead individuals to correct beliefs. At present, philosophy has little

Astronomers at work with a quadrant (left) and a telescope (right) at the Royal Observatory, Greenwich, Eng., founded by John Flamsteed in 1675. Trustees of the Science Museum, London

by way of data on which to build. It is already possible, however, to envisage a future philosophical account that avoids the limitations of the individualistic perspective now current.

Such an account might find that the social structures inherited from the early-modern period are quite satisfactory as a means of pursuing the aims of the sciences (although that would be surprising). Some contemporary philosophers believe that good reasons for thinking this will not be so are already apparent. Pointing to the exclusion, or marginalization, of some groups of people, they suggest that the current collective practice of science is biased toward the realization of a partial set of values. The most vigorous articulation of this perspective is offered in recent feminist philosophy of science.

FEMINIST THEMES

There are various ways of pursuing feminist themes in connection with the sciences. An important project, often dismissed as too limited, is to document the ways in which women have been excluded from participation in research projects. More philosophically ambitious is the attempt to show how women's exclusion led to a bias in the conclusions that scientists accept. Here there is a classic and compelling example: during the 1950s and '60s, (male) primatologists arrived at hypotheses about territoriality and aggression in the troops of primates they studied; as an increasing number of women entered the field in the 1970s, aspects of primate social life that had been invisible came to be noted, and the old hypotheses were forced to undergo radical revision. The specific moral of this case is that pooling the observations of both men and women may enlarge the range of evidence available to the scientific community; the more general point is that a diversity of social backgrounds and social roles can sometimes provide the most inclusive body of data.

Feminists sometimes wanted to argue for a bolder thesis. Appealing to the general thesis of the underdetermination of theories by evidence, they claimed that choices between equally good rivals are made by introducing considerations of value that reflect the masculine bias of the scientific community. Yet this style of argument works no better in this context than it did in the blanket sociological invocation of underdetermination considered

Jane Goodall studying a baboon in 1974. A rise in the number of active female primatologists in the 1970s caused a reexamination of scientific conclusions in the field from decades before. **Fotos International/Archive Photos/Getty Images**

in the last section. Where feminists can make a detailed case for the existence of equivalent rivals, it is important to probe their decision making to see whether an arbitrary choice is being grounded in a problematic way. There is no general reason for believing that evidential considerations always fall short, creating a vacuum that can be filled only by the irruption of masculine values.

The feminist argument does, however, point toward a deeper issue. Once it is understood that science is a social enterprise, it may be supposed that the institutions that guide the development of the sciences absorb major features of the background society, including the privileged position of men, and that this affects the goals set for the sciences and the values placed on certain types of scientific achievements. This form of the feminist critique is extremely important in bringing into the open issues that have been neglected in traditional philosophy of science. They can best be approached by returning to the unfinished question of the nature of scientific progress.

PROGRESS AND VALUES

Suppose that scientific realism succeeds in fighting off challenges to the view that the sciences attain (or accumulate, or converge on) truth. Does this mean that there is now a satisfactory understanding of scientific progress as increasing grasp of truth? Not necessarily. For the truths about nature are too many, and most of them are not worth knowing. Even if one focuses on a small region of the universe—a particular room, say, during the period of an hour—there are infinitely many languages for describing that room and, for each such language, infinitely many true statements about the room during that time.

Simply accumulating truth about the world is far too easy. Scientific progress would not be made by dispatching armies of investigators to count leaves or grains of sand. If the sciences make progress, it is because they offer an increasing number of significant truths about the world.

The question of scientific progress is unfinished because this notion of significance was not sufficiently analyzed. Many philosophers wrote either as if the aim of the sciences is to deliver the complete truth about the world (a goal that is not obviously coherent and is surely unattainable) or as if there is some objective notion of significance, given by nature. What might this notion of significance be? Perhaps that the truths desired are the laws of nature or the fundamental principles that govern natural phenomena. But proposals like this are vulnerable to the worries about the role of laws and the possibility of unified science. Moreover, many thriving sciences do not seem to be in the business of enunciating laws; there appear to be large obstacles to finding some "theory of everything" that will integrate and subsume all the sciences that have been pursued (let alone those that might be pursued in the future). A sober look at the variety of scientific research undertaken today suggests that the sciences seek true answers to questions that are taken to be significant, either because they arouse people's curiosity or because they lend themselves to the pursuit of practical goals that people want to achieve. The agenda for research is set not by nature but by society.

At this point, the feminist critique obtains a purchase, for the picture just outlined identifies judgments of value as central to the direction of scientific inquiry—we pursue the truths that matter to us. But who are the "we" whose values enter into the identification of the goals of the sciences? To what extent do the value judgments actually made leave out important constituencies within the human population? These are serious questions, and one of the main contributions of feminist philosophy of science is to bring them to philosophical attention.

The main point, however, is general. An account of the goals of science cannot rest with the bare assertion that the sciences seek truth. Philosophers should offer an analysis of which kinds of truths are important, and, unless they can revive the idea of an "objective agenda set by nature," they will have to conclude that judgments about human interests and values are part of a philosophical account of science. This means that philosophy of science can no longer confine itself to treating issues that relate to logic, epistemology, and metaphysics (questions about the reconstruction of scientific theories, the nature of natural necessity, and the conditions under which hypotheses are confirmed). Moral and political philosophy will also enter the philosophy of science.

Insofar as philosophers have reflected on the ethics of science, they have often regarded the questions as relatively straightforward. Application of virtually any major moral theory will support restrictions on the kinds of things that can be done to people in scientific experimentation; everyday maxims about honesty will generate the conclusions about fraud and misrepresentation that are routinely made when cases of scientific misconduct surface. These issues about the ways in which scientists are expected to behave in their daily work are superficial; the deeper moral and political questions concern the ways in which the goals of inquiry are set (and, correspondingly, in which progress is understood). One might say, vaguely, that the sciences should pursue those truths whose attainment would best promote the collective good; but this, of course, leaves the hard philosophical task of understanding "the collective good." How should the divergent interests of different groups of people be weighed? How should the balance between satisfying human curiosity and solving practical problems be struck? How should future gains be judged in relation to short-term demands? Philosophy of science has so far said too little in response to these questions.

Many of the philosophical topics so clearly formulated by the logical positivists and logical empiricists are, rightly, still the focus of 21st-century concern. Increased understanding of the history of the sciences and of the social character of scientific practice has set broader tasks for the philosophy of science. In a world in which the power of scientific research, for good and for ill, is becoming increasingly obvious, it is to be hoped that issues about the values adopted in the pursuit of science will become more central to philosophical discussion.

A ristotle was one of the greatest intellectual figures of Western history. He was the author of a philosophical and scientific system that became the framework and vehicle for both Christian Scholasticism and medieval Islamic philosophy. Even after the intellectual revolutions of the Renaissance, the Reformation, and the Enlightenment, Aristotelian concepts remained embedded in Western thinking.

Today Aristotle can be described as both a philosopher and a scientist. Yet he himself likely would not have drawn a distinction between those two roles—nor, until the 19th century, when the modern sense of *science* began to take hold, would many other people. Since the early 20th century, however, the philosophy of science has been more self-conscious about its proper role in the realm of scientific inquiry. Some philosophers continue to work on problems that are continuous with the natural sciences, exploring, for example, the character of space and time or the fundamental features of life. They contribute to the philosophy of the special sciences, a field with a long tradition of distinguished work in the philosophy of physics and with more-recent contributions in the philosophy of biology and the philosophy of psychology and neuroscience. Today, there are also those who are dedicated to a general philosophy of science and who seek to illuminate broad features of the sciences, continuing the inquiries begun in Aristotle's discussions of logic and method.

algorithm A step-by-step procedure for solving a problem or accomplishing some end, typically involving repetition of an operation.

axiom An established rule or principle or a self-evident truth.

cognitive Based on or capable of being reduced to factual knowledge based on observation.

empiricism The practice of relying on observation and experiment especially in the natural sciences.

hypothetico-deductive A method of testing hypotheses by determining whether their logical consequences are consistent with observed data.

inference The act of passing from statistical sample data to generalizations, usually with calculated degrees of certainty.

plausible Superficially fair, reasonable, or valuable, often deceptively so.

premise A proposition supposed or proved on the basis of argument or inference.

probability The chance that an event is likely to occur.

protocol A detailed plan of a scientific or medical experiment, treatment, or procedure.

qualitative Of or relating to quality or kind.

quantitative Expressible in terms of quantity.

subjective Of or relating to the essential being of that which has substance, qualities, attributes, or relations.

tractable Capable of being easily led, taught, or contolled.

CLASSIC TEXTS

Many classic articles in the logical empiricist tradition can be found in Carl G. Hempel, *Aspects of Scientific Explanation, and Other Essays in the Philosophy of Science* (1965); the standard textbooks in this tradition are Carl G. Hempel, *Philosophy of Natural Science* (1966); and, at a more advanced level, Ernest Nagel, *The Structure of Science: Problems in the Logic of Scientific Explanation*, 2nd ed. (1979). An extremely influential monograph read in many different disciplines and contexts is Thomas S. Kuhn, *The Structure of Scientific Revolutions*, 4th ed. (2012).

CONTEMPORARY LOGICAL EMPIRICISM

A thorough empiricist approach to issues about confirmation is John Earman, *Bayes or Bust?: A Critical Examination of Bayesian Confirmation Theory* (1992). Scientific explanation is treated in Wesley C. Salmon, *Scientific Explanation and the Causal Structure of the World* (1984), and *Causality and Explanation* (1998). A valuable anthology of essays on this topic is Joseph Pitt (ed.), *Scientific Explanation* (1986). Bas C. van Fraassen, *The Scientific Image* (1980), and *Laws and Symmetry* (1989), discuss issues about theories and scientific laws. These issues are also discussed from a different perspective in Ronald Giere, *Explaining Science* (1988).

SCIENTIFIC CHANGE AND SCIENTIFIC REALISM

The questions raised by Thomas Kuhn are taken up in Larry Laudan, *Progress and Its Problems: Toward a Theory of Scientific Growth* (1977); and Philip Kitcher, *The Advancement of Science: Science Without Legend, Objectivity Without Illusions* (1993). The latter book also responds to the more radical sociohistorical perspective offered in David Bloor, *Knowledge and Social Imagery*, 2nd ed. (1991); and Steven Shapin and Simon Schaffer, *Leviathan and the Air-Pump: Hobbes, Boyle, and the Experimental Life* (1985). David Papineau (ed.), *Philosophy of Science* (1996), is a collection of major articles on scientific realism.

THE DISUNITY OF SCIENCE

Challenges to logical empiricist ideas about the unity of science are mounted in Nancy Cartwright, *The Dappled World: A Study of the Boundaries of Science* (1999); and John Dupré, *The Disorder of Things: Metaphysical Foundations of the Disunity of Science* (1993).

SCIENCE AND SOCIETY

A classic discussion of social aspects of scientific inquiry is Helen E. Longino, *Science as Social Knowledge: Values and Objectivity in Scientific Inquiry* (1990). A different perspective on this topic, much neglected in traditional philosophy of science, is given in Philip Kitcher, *Science, Truth, and Democracy* (2001).